For Paint

This little horse had a heart as big as Texas.
He is mentioned in several places in this book.

I first saw him when he belonged to Apache.
When the pony was 9, Apache sold him to me.
He died at age 23 while I was writing this book.

He was one little paint horse that
always
made you pay attention.

TIED HARD AND FAST

APACHE ADAMS - BIG BEND COWBOY

BY DON CADDEN

Outskirts Press, Inc.
Denver, Colorado

Tied Hard and Fast
Apache Adams - Big Bend Cowboy
All Rights Reserved.
Copyright © 2011 Don Cadden
v3.0

Cover Design by Melissa Cadden.
Permission has been granted for the use of all stories and photographs in this book.

Don Cadden
HC 65, Box 28-V
Alpine, TX 79830
dcadden@gmail.com
www.dcadden.com

Outskirts Press, Inc.
http://www.outskirtspress.com

ISBN: 978-1-4327-7117-1

Outskirts Press and the "OP" logo are trademarks belonging to Outskirts Press, Inc.

PRINTED IN THE UNITED STATES OF AMERICA

Apache Adams ahorseback, 1980s

One Hell of a Cowboy

I guess I'm one of the luckiest fellers alive. I've pretty much done something I've enjoyed for a living every day of my life. I've been married to the same woman for over 50 years and still love her to death. I've had good horses, good friends, good times, and very few regrets.

It's been a wild ride with a lot of broken bones and a few heart-aches; but I wouldn't change much, and I'd do it all again if I could. I want to spend my last day on earth ahorseback, and the only thing I want on my tombstone is "Apache Adams, One Hell of a Cowboy."

—Apache Adams

Contents

Dedication: For Paint
One Hell of a Cowboy

PART ONE
NOTHIN' BUT A COWBOY
Apache's Early Life and Experiences

CHAPTER 1   GROWING UP ON THE RIVER 1
   Uncle Elba's Bronc 6
   Skunking My Brother 8
   Little Vaquero 10
   I Rode Him a Jump-and-a-Half 11
   Bad Mules and High Water 13
   One Tough Hombre 14

CHAPTER 2   LEAVING HOME 17
   Graduating a Little Early 17
   Lighting Up the Day Hands 18
   Shoot Him Again 19
   Smuggling a Dead Man 20
   Wild Jackasses 21
   Love of My Life 22
   Spilled Milk 25
   Fast Gun 26
   Losing Dad 27
   Life on the River 29
   Sul Ross Horses 31
   Boquillas Canyon 32
   Tennis Shoes and a Winchester Rifle 34
   Oops, Wrong Judge 36

CHAPTER 3   LIFE IN THE BIG CITY **39**

My Kind of School 40

Till You Run Out of Horses or Money 42

Shoeing in the Rain 44

CHAPTER 4   BACK TO THE BIG BEND **45**

Home from Houston 45

Credit at the Bank 47

Paybacks 48

Another Damn Milk Cow 49

Running Out of Rope 51

Banana Bull 52

Kentucky Fried Adams 54

Bad Dreams and Buttermilk 55

More Crazy Cows 57

Bucking Horses and Arrowheads 58

Pump Jack 60

Big Gray 62

Hanging Domingo 63

Flying High 64

Full of Bull 65

Gary 66

CHAPTER 5   INTO THE '80s AND BEYOND **69**

Big Bucks in the Fur Business 69

Closed Range 70

Ray Hunt 72

Catch 22 73

Roping a Mountain Lion 74

Teaching a Horse to Fly—Almost 75

Making New Cowboys 78

From Stockbroker to Cowboy 80

Mad Cow 81

Pushing on the Reins 82

Pinto Canyon 86

Roping a Saddle 89
Tired Bull... 91
Down South with Ben Benavides.. 92
Wreck in the Kitchen 93
Stripping the Inspector Down 94
Legal Cattle Rustling 96
Stinkin' Goats and Broken Bones 100
Where Am I?... 102
The Wild and Wooly 02 Ranch 103
New Ranch, More Broken Bones.. 106

PART TWO
HE'LL DO TO RIDE THE RIVER WITH
The Author's Experiences Riding with Apache Adams

Butch & Sundance 111
The Real Deal.. 112
Grub and Wood Stoves.. 114
Lost Horses... 116
Bucked Off 118
Almost Bucked Off 119
Swimming the Rio Grande... 121
Loud Horse Whispering 123
Shootin' the Bull... 124
Wild Bulls and Deer Feeders 128
Roping Cows in Town 130

PART THREE
RECOLLECTIONS
Stories from a Few Friends

Stanza from "The Zebra Dun"... 137
Joe Richardson.. 139
Steve Stumberg... 140

Dusty Roller 142
Pat Yeager 144
Frankie Galvan 144
David Adams 146
Preston Adams 148
Ted Gray 149

EPILOGUE 151

ACKNOWLEDGEMENTS 153

ABOUT THE AUTHOR 155

Photographs

1. Apache Adams ahorseback, 1980s v

2. Ulice and Mildred Adams at The River Ranch 3

3. Left to right, in front: Ulice Adams, Shipwreck, Apache Adams,
    and Billie Burleson, In back: David Burleson and Mildred
    Adams 5

4. Adams chuckwagon at a 4th of July Celebration. A young
    Apache is on the right in the black hat 8

5. Kids on the Rio Grande. Preston Adams is second from the left;
    Apache is second from the right 9

6. Apache and two ranch hands 12

7. Apache and Joy Adams in the 1950s 24

8. Burros loaded with candelilla wax 37

9. Apache and Bob Gerkin taking a break at Bob's horsehoeing
    school in Houston, 1964 41

10. Working cattle at The River Ranch pens 56

11. Grandson Dusty ahorseback at age 4-1/2 80

12. Remuda in The River Ranch pens during the Wild Burro Gathering, mid-1990s. Notice "Car Mountain" in the background 83

13. Apache winning the buckle at The Wild Burro Gathering at The River Ranch, mid-1990s.. 84

14. Rope-off for the burro-gathering buckle. Apache is second from the left; he won the buckle 85

15. Apache riding Dunny at a roping 99

16. Apache and Joy Adams, 2009.. 107

17. The author and Apache working cattle, 2010........................ 113

18. The author and Apache in the middle of the Rio Grande near The River Ranch, late 1990s 120

19. Apache showing Jeff Fort and the author the trail to Marufo Vega that he traveled regularly as a kid 122

20. Blain Ward sitting on the tied-down bull that he tried to shoot with a tranquilizer gun, "Buffalo Bill style" 126

21. Apache (in the black hat) being inducted into The Big Bend Cowboy Hall of Fame in 2009 133

22. Branding crew on the Adams Ranch, circa 2009; left to right: Blain Ward, the author, Pat Yeager, Dusty Roller, Frankie Galvan, Justin Clinton, Apache (nursing a broken pelvis) 141

23. Apache heeling a calf at Adams Ranch branding, 2010. Grandson Dusty waiting to flank the calf 143

24. Frankie Galvan and Apache ahorseback, 2010 145

25. Don Cadden, the author 155

PART ONE
NOTHIN' BUT A COWBOY

Apache's Early Life
and Experiences

CHAPTER **1**

GROWING UP ON THE RIVER

The mule had his head between his front feet, and his hind feet were headed for the moon.

My dad, Ulice Adams, was hanging on with one spur hooked on the swell of the saddle while his head bounced off the mule's butt. He somehow managed to pull himself back up into the saddle, only to have to save himself again by grabbing the horn as the mule changed directions and bucked sideways. He finally got the mule's head up and got him slowed to a crow-hop before he was able to trot him over to his brother, Elba.

"By God, Ulice, that mule had you bucked clean off three different times," chuckled my uncle Elba. "I'm still not sure how you rode him."

"Well, Elby," Dad said, "I never could see no good place to land, so I just had to hang on."

It was the mid-1940s, but it might as well have been the mid-1840s as far as my dad and Uncle Elba were concerned. They were living and ranching in the rugged, wild country known as the Big Bend of Texas. It was 75 miles by dirt road to the little town of Marathon, and you still weren't anywhere when you got there.

They had moved out of the tents they had lived in for several years and into what they called the "grass house," a hovel built from yucca and sotol stalks. Electricity wouldn't come to this part of the country until 1957, and along with it a way to keep food fresh in the miserable hot summers like we have around there.

Drinking water wasn't a problem; we just hauled water up to the house from the nearby Rio Grande and stored it in big barrels. At night, the chickens liked to roost on the water barrels, so one of us kids had to be the "chicken turner" and keep turning the birds tail-out, so they didn't do their business in the water.

Most everything on the ranch was done "ahorseback," which suited us just fine.

There was one old car, but neither Dad nor Uncle Elba cared much for driving it. If Dad was driving, he just lined the big radiator cap up with the line down the middle of the highway and let other folks work around him.

Dad had married my mother, Mildred Babb, in 1927 in Juno, Texas, a little place south of Ozona and Sonora on Devils River.

She had been raised in West Texas, in fact had been born in the old Judge Roy Bean Saloon in Langtry, which had been converted into living quarters. The Babbs owned most of Langtry and had the reputation of being folks who stood their ground.

Mother and Dad had been given several hundred goats as a wedding gift. In 1930, they walked a couple of hundred miles herding the goats on foot, and moved all of them to Harmon Adams' ranch, Dad's uncle, near Devils River.

Over the next several years, they worked on various ranches and put what extra money they could toward building their own herd. At one point, they lived in a tent in what is now Big Bend National Park and worked for Mother's uncle, Boye Babb, taking care of his goats.

One of their jobs was to ride ahorseback around the mountain rims and keep pushing the goats down to the lower country. If they weren't trying to keep those old bronc horses from bucking off the edge of a cliff, they were trying to run the mountain lions off the nanny goats.

Many years later, I gave a talk at Big Bend Park, telling a bunch of city folks how Mother and Dad "threw the goats off the top of those mountains."

Afterwards, the head ranger that was putting on the program came over and said, "Mr. Adams, you've sure upset some of the ladies that were listening to your stories today."

I couldn't imagine what I'd done and asked him what the problem was.

"Oh," he said, "they just couldn't believe your parents would be so cruel as to throw those poor little goats off the side of the mountains. Why would they do that?"

Ulice and Mildred Adams at The River Ranch

I had to go explain to those women that when cowboys talk about throwing a bunch of cattle together or throwing goats off the side of a mountain, it just meant they moved them. Mother and Dad didn't really pick them up and throw them off the mountain!

Anyway, in the midst of all the work and the goat-throwing, Mother and Dad managed to have a daughter, Eula Mae, and then a son, Delbert. Delbert was later taken by disease at age 6.

Then in late August of 1937, mother took the train to her mother's home in Del Rio to await the birth of another child. On September 11ᵗʰ, she gave birth to her second son.

Dad got word and a couple of days later arrived in Del Rio to see his new boy. He pulled the blanket back to take a peek and saw a healthy little fellow with coal black hair growing all the way down his neck to his back. With a grunt he said, "Looks like a little Apache Indian to me."

The name stuck, and even though Mother recorded my name on the birth certificate as Ernest Paul Adams, I've always been "Apache." If somebody calls my house wanting to speak to Ernest, I know it's either the law or an insurance salesman.

Mother, Dad, Uncle Elba, and his wife Buddie were plenty tough folks and were living and ranching in some of the roughest country anywhere. Being on the border with Mexico added to the problems; several other fellers before them had failed on the same land they were working.

One day while he was in Marathon picking up supplies, Dad stopped into a local bar to enjoy a rare cold beer.

A group of local ranchers was sitting around a table drinking, and one of them asked, "Ain't you the young feller who bought that old ranch down by Stillwells?"

When Dad said he was, the man replied, "So what makes you think you can make a go of it when a bunch of other men couldn't?"

Dad looked at the man and said, "Well, for one thing, I plan on running it from ahorseback, not from one of these beer joints in town."

He did, too, and with a little luck and a lot of work made a good go of it and raised our family there. They added horses and cattle to the goat operation. The damn coyotes and mountain lions did their best to drive them out of business, but they survived in some of the hardest country imaginable.

Left to right, in front: Ulice Adams, Shipwreck, Apache Adams,
and Billie Burleson
In back: David Burleson and Mildred Adams

Living on what they named The River Ranch, our families enjoyed the freedom and beauty of a way of life that was becoming rare in the 20th century. Even in the 1940s, there were fewer and fewer places where people worked ahorseback every day, drank from the river, cooked on wood stoves, and read by coal oil lamps.

The Rio Grande was the legal boundary between the U.S. and Mexico, but it wasn't much more than a belly-deep ride ahorseback and sure didn't mean much to the folks who lived on either side of it in the Big Bend.

Across the river was a small village, and then the larger village of Boquillas was upriver a few miles.

The villages had some good *vaqueros* who were looking for work, and we Adams could always use good, cheap help. We had good business relations and friendships; and aside from family, these

Mexicanos were the mainstay as ranch hands and other help for lots of years.

I was ahorseback, riding with one of my folks, before I could walk. The Rio Grande was a place to get a drink and swim, and something to cross when you wanted to play with other kids. When I learned an English word, I learned the Spanish word, too.

When I was big enough, about age 6 or 7, to work with the branding crews, Dad sent me out with one of the top hands. I learned to track from men who were as much Indio as Mexican. I learned the ways of the *vaquero* from men whose ancestors hadn't known any other way of life since the Spanish brought cattle to the New World.

With screw worms[1] still real bad in all the livestock, there weren't many days that something didn't have to be roped so we could treat it. And with Dad sometimes running as many as 500 brood mares, there were always horses and mules to break and plenty of young horses to ride.

All of this, and my desire to be nothing but a cowboy, led to a pretty interesting life.

Uncle Elba's Bronc

Back in the mid-'40s, the cavalry had pretty much quit using horses and weren't buying them like they used to, so horses got pretty cheap. My dad Ulice bought a bunch of mares at a good price over in Dryden.

Instead of spending the money trucking them to the ranch, he decided we'd herd them. It was about 130 miles cross-country to the ranch, and we had to go through part of Mexico.

I was about 8 or 9 years old when my dad, my uncle Elba, my cousin Preston, and I drove over to Dryden.

---

1   screw worms - The larva of a parasitic fly that has been laid in any type of open wound. The fly was finally eradicated in the U.S. in the late '60s. Because this type of fly only breeds once in its lifetime, airplane crews dropped boxes of sterile flies that bred with existing flies. Thus, fly hatches were eliminated. Prior to that, animals had to be constantly monitored and treated for worms in even the smallest wound.

A feller there named Burt Becket had two old gentle mules in the pen, so Preston and I saddled them up and gathered the horses out of the horse trap[2] and put them in the pens. Burt said he was keeping all the saddle horses but would sell Dad the mares and colts and the two mules.

There was one mare that was broke to ride, and Dad reached out and roped her real quick. There was a dun[3] gelding about four years old in with the mares, and he'd never even had a rope on him, much less a saddle. Dad hollered, "O hell, I'm sure Elby can ride him!"

Dad and Uncle Elba fore-footed[4] him, got him down, got a hackamore[5] on him, tied his foot up, and got a saddle on him. Uncle Elba got on him and just let him run around in among those mares and colts for a few minutes.

Finally, we opened the gate and turned the horses out on a dirt road going toward Mexico.

Dad and Preston and I just tried to keep Uncle Elba thrown in with the bunch of horses because he sure didn't have much steering on that unbroken horse. In a couple of hours, that old horse settled down and quit trying to throw a fit and trotted along pretty good with the other horses.

When we got to the river, there were cane breaks real thick on both sides. We hobbled our saddle horses and just let the others run loose. We camped in the middle of the trail, so the horses couldn't go back home.

The next morning we saddled up, Uncle Elba saddling his bronc without much trouble, and drove them to Rancho Nuevo over in Mexico. We borrowed some horse-shoeing equipment from the cowboys there and shod Dad and Uncle Elba's horses.

The following morning we headed home to the ranch. We were on the trail for three days; and by the time we got home, that dun

---

2   horse trap – A pasture used to keep horses in so they can be easily gathered.
3   dun - A yellowish tan-colored horse, sometimes with a dark line down its back.
4   fore-foot – To rope a horse's front foot in order to throw it to the ground.
5   hackamore - A type of bridle, usually used on a young or unbroken horse, that doesn't have a bit that goes into the horse's mouth. Controls the head and nose without bothering the mouth.

horse was pretty well broke...well, at least what we called "broke" back then.

Adams chuckwagon at a 4th of July Celebration.
A young Apache is on the right in the black hat.

Skunking My Brother

When we were kids, my brother David and I kept traps out all winter. One time, our cousin Preston came to visit, and we all went to check the traps.

We had a polecat[6] caught in one of the traps. Skunk pelts were bringing about 50 cents apiece, so we killed that one and skinned it. 'Course, we got sprayed pretty good, but that wasn't any big deal to some serious 8-year-old trappers.

While we were scouting around the trap, we heard something. We looked up under a rock ledge and found a whole mess of baby polecats. We figured we'd hit the jackpot. Since David was a couple of years younger than Preston and me, we talked him into reaching in and catching them.

---

6   polecat – A skunk.

We convinced him that if he grabbed them real quick and held their tail down, they couldn't spray him. So David reached in, grabbed one, and shoved his tail down. But the skunk got him right in the face.

He went to squalling and had that ol' yellow skunk spray all over his face.

We got him calmed down and told him that he just nearly got it done, but he needed to be a little quicker. We talked him into pulling four little polecats out from under that ledge before we finished.

We skinned them all, but Mother and Dad wouldn't let us in the house for several days after that.

Kids on the Rio Grande.
Preston Adams is second from the left;
Apache is second from the right.

Little Vaquero

My dad had about 200,000 acres of the Black Gap Game Preserve leased for cattle and horses at a nickel an acre. He had a crew of men that stayed out there full-time.

They would ride around the dirt tanks[7] and catch any little calves that needed branding and doctor everything for screw worms. They made a big circle of the tanks on that place and stayed out all the time.

When I got out of school at the end of May, Dad's cow boss Lalo Lopez would be waiting for me with a good kid horse, and I'd stay with the *vaqueros* most of the summer.

These fellers were salt-of-the-earth cowboys, and my Spanish got better because they didn't speak any English. We mostly ate tortillas and beans, with a little beef sometimes; the only thing we had to drink was coffee and water. We slept on the ground with just our old saddle blankets for bedding and seldom changed clothes or bathed. That was pretty good experience for a 7-, 8-, 9-year-old kid.

Dad had an uncle, Harmon Adams, who had a ranch about 30 miles south of Van Horn. He loved to hoorah[8] kids, and we all loved him. One year when I was about 10 years old, I went to stay with him for a couple of weeks.

I thought I was a full-grown cowboy by then, so my dad took my leggings[9], bridle, spurs, and saddle and sewed everything up in a big gunny sack. We loaded it on the bus, and I made the 130-mile trip from Marathon to Van Horn. Uncle Harmon met me at the bus station, and we went down to his ranch.

When we'd go to town, he'd tell me all these stories about the Headless Horseman riding silently through the night looking for little cow punchers or about bears that killed men and rode off on the men's horses, carrying the dead fellers across the saddle. He had me so scared I wouldn't even get out and open the gates if it was dark.

7   dirt tank - Also called stock tank; a small man-made reservoir used to water livestock.
8   hoorah -(HOO-rah) - Old cowboy term for teasing someone.
9   leggings - Chaps made of leather worn to protect the rider's legs from brush and thorns.

Several years later, Uncle Harmon got into some trouble with the U.S. government for bringing horses out of Mexico without the proper paperwork. He had horses scattered all around and south of Van Horn.

My dad, uncle, cousin, and I went over to try and gather them for him. We were going to drive them from the Van Horn area all the way to our place 70 miles south of Marathon.

When we got there the first morning, Dad sent my cousin and me out to jingle the horses[10] out of about a two-section[11] horse trap. Uncle Harmon had told Dad all the horses in the trap were good, gentle saddle horses. I noticed a little bob-tailed roan horse in the bunch and told my dad I wanted to ride him.

We spent about a week gathering horses.

On the third or fourth day Uncle Harmon showed up. He said he'd forgotten to tell Dad to be sure and not let one of the kids on that little roan horse because he was really bad to pitch and kind of an outlaw.

Dad said, "Harmon, you're a little late. Apache's been riding him for the last three days."

That horse had never given me a bit of trouble, and he was my top horse for about the next ten years.

I Rode Him a Jump-and-a-Half

Back in the early '50s, we ran about 1,000 head of cattle and 500 head of mares in the Black Gap Game Preserve area. We were using those old government re-mount studs on the mares. We had a crew of five Mexican men who were breaking those horses.

They would ride them a couple of months and then turn them back out. Once a year in April, we'd gather the horses we wanted to sell; and my cousin, my brother, and I would drive them to town. When we were starting off with that big remuda[12] towards Marathon

---

10   jingle horses - To gather and bring in the horse herd, usually before daylight. A jingle horse is usually kept up at night for this purpose.
11   section - One square mile (640 acres) of land.
12   remuda – A Spanish term for a group of horses; also called a "cavy."

one cool morning, I was riding a big horse named Oscar.

He was fresh and feeling pretty good, enjoying the nip in the air and ready to go somewhere. He kept trying to go in with the herd instead of staying back like we were supposed to. I had to keep pulling him up and making him wait, and I guess he got enough of it and went to bucking pretty good.

He bucked me off and then turned and ran back to the pens. About a half-mile.

When Dad saw my horse without me on him, he jumped in the truck and drove up to the herd to see what had happened.

Apache and two ranch hands

I came running up to him and said, "Dad, you'd be proud! I rode him a whole jump-and-a-half!"

It took us two days to drive the horses 70 miles into the stock pens in Marathon. That was some rough old country, and we had our hands full keeping those horses from grazing all day on what little grass there was.

At night, we just slept on our saddle blankets under the big West Texas sky. I don't think any place in the world has stars and a night sky like West Texas. And when the sun goes down it gets pretty chilly in the desert.

In Marathon, Dad hired several good cowboys to ride the horses from the stock pens in front of Richey's store up to the Chambers Hotel. They'd lope them up there and then turn and walk and trot them back to kind of show them off.

Ranches like the Gage, the o6, and Combs Cattle Company and some of the small sheep and goat outfits would come in and bid on our horses. We'd sell 70 or 80 head of horses a year like that.

Along about 1952 or '53, it got so dry that the horses really hung close to the Rio Grande, and they would cross back and forth.

The river riders were down there then and didn't like it when the horses crossed. It was their job to keep all animals from crossing back and forth across the border and transporting diseases into the U.S. from Mexico.

We made two big gathers and took all those horses up to Marathon. There, Dad sold them to Indio Calzada, who shipped them to a buyer in Louisiana.

Bad Mules and High Water

Back before Dad shipped all those horses, we had a bunch of mules because the sheep and goat ranchers really liked to use good mules. When our men were breaking horses, they always had a couple of mules apiece to break, too.

No sooner had Dad sold all our broke mules than an outfit from over in Ft. Davis called and said they needed about five or six good saddle mules. They offered Dad a premium for them.

It was around Cinco de Mayo[13], and all his regular bronc riders

---

13   Cinco de Mayo – A Mexican holiday on the 5th of May.

were gone home to Mexico for a week; so Dad called George and Estus, his two brothers from Dryden, to come help him.

They gathered up about six mules and started breaking them for those folks. They'd ride them a couple of miles every morning and then make a couple of mile circles on them every evening. My uncles rode them for a couple of weeks like that, and then they loaded them in a bob-tailed truck with wood side boards.

Dad always said that you didn't want to get a mule real tired when you were first starting them. He said if you got them tired and sweating behind the ears when you were starting them, that's when they would pick up bad tricks and habits.

They started to town with them and got to Maravillas Creek. It was up and running big. By then, the creek behind them had come up, too, and they couldn't go back to the ranch; so they camped there for the night. Out in our country, the sky can be crystal clear and blue; but if it's raining 70 or 80 miles away, you might have the roads blocked from the runoff.

When they got up the next morning, the mules had just about eaten through all of the oak side boards on the truck.

The men had to cut mesquite limbs and tie them to the side boards to keep the mules in. They ran into more high water that slowed them down some more.

By the time they got into town, they had limbs and trees tied all over that truck.

But they got $125 apiece for the mules.

One Tough Hombre

When I was about 15 years old, we were running a lot of cattle down on the Rio Grande. Some of our cattle would cross over into Mexico, and some of the neighbor's Mexican cattle would cross over on our side.

So when the Mexicans would work cattle, Dad would send me over for 4 or 5 days to help and bring any of our cattle back.

The Mexican *vaqueros* all used 60-foot maguey ropes[14], and dallied on those old wooden saddle horns.

The cowboys would play whatever they roped like a fish, letting out rope and then taking it back up because those ropes weren't very strong and would break if they weren't careful.

They'd let that rope slide and burn, and smoke would boil up from those slick wood saddle horns. When the cow would stop, they'd take the slack back up and do it again.

We were working by a big stock tank one day, marking and branding calves.

One old cow had a horn growing into her head, and the cow boss told a couple of his men to head-and-heel her so that one of the men on the ground could cut the horn off.

While one feller headed her, a fairly young cowboy heeled her and got his little finger caught between the rope and the saddle horn. When the rope started sliding, it just cut that finger off at the joint like a knife through hot butter. He had skin and leaders hanging out the end of his finger.

One of those old hands saw what happened and jerked that young feller off his horse and pulled him over to the branding fire.

Several fellers held him while another cowboy stuck a hot branding iron to it. I can still smell his hide burning and hear him squealing and hollering when they hit him with that iron, but he finally settled down.

Of course they didn't have any kind of painkiller, not even aspirin.

That night, one of the older *vaqueros* took some leather and made a little sleeve to fit over the part of the finger he had left. He took some cotton out of an old mattress and stuck in the end of the sleeve.

The next morning that boy was back out there working with us. He never missed a minute's work. I always figured that was one of the toughest ol' kids I'd ever seen.

---

14   maguey rope – A rope made from the fiber of the maguey plant.

CHAPTER 2

LEAVING HOME

Graduating a Little Early

I mainly went to school so I could play six-man football, and because my folks made me. In March, right before I was supposed to graduate from high school in May, I got in a disagreement with one of the teachers and decked him. He dang sure deserved it, but that ended my school career, so I went to hunting a job.

I was over in Pecos, and somebody told me about an old man who was hiring; they said he'd hire anyone that would work, "but you damn sure had to work." They said he had come into town and was down at the domino hall.

So I looked him up down there and introduced myself to Mr. Joe Rounsaville, who owned The KC Ranch. He told me I would have to work, and I'd have to ride young horses.

I told him that wasn't a problem, that I was used to both, so that afternoon, I got in the truck with him, and he took me to the headquarters ranch up near Balmorhea. I worked on and off for him for the next few years. _Billie Birnios hometown_

Back then, there was a constant problem with screw worms in cattle and horses. Baby calves would get them in their navel; calves would get them in a fresh brand or where they'd been castrated. So every day, you were roping stock and doctoring screw worms. All of those old horses were used to stopping and facing livestock when you got something roped.

Right after I went to work there, we were gathering a bunch of wild mares. The horses at the KCs kinda had a reputation for being a little inbred and being bad to pitch and kick. I was riding a horse that morning named Diablo that was no exception.

We were working a 50-section pasture and had gathered most of the horses, but we were having to go back and rope the ones we couldn't gather. Some of the boys were running a little bunch of horses toward me, so I picked out one and took off across a big flat, building a loop to rope him.

I'd just stood up to throw when my horse hit a hole and turned a flip. I was tied on hard and fast to the horn; and when the horse fell, the rope wrapped and tightened around my arm.

The horse just rolled and was on his feet headed straight for those wild horses in a run.

I was being drug but was able to get my other hand on the rope so it didn't tear my arm off. There's probably nothing a cowboy dreads more than being drug, and this definitely had my full attention.

Just before Diablo got to a big cedar thicket, I guess he felt something pulling hard on the rope and turned to face me. He'd drug me about 100 yards, and I was damn glad to be loose from him.

I was able to get the rope off my hand. Besides my leggings being torn almost off along with some of my hide, I wasn't too much worse for the wear.

Lighting Up the Day Hands

Back then, I was making about $4.00 a day working full time for the KCs. When they hired day hands during the round ups, they paid them $8.00 a day. And the day hands got to ride the horses that we had already broken and trained.

So another regular hand and I decided we'd fix those fellers up good. It was our job to start a bunch of young horses after the fall and spring works and to have them pretty well broke when the next works started.

He and I didn't smoke, but most everybody did in those days. We each got us a shirt pocket full of big kitchen matches. We'd be riding along on those young horses and strike a match on top of the screw on the saddle horn like the smokers did. Just as we'd strike the match, we'd rake the horse with our spurs and get 'em pitching or let 'em run off.

The next spring those day hands would ride out in the morning, and in a little bit they'd roll a cigarette and reach down and pop that match off the saddle horn. When they did, those horses would break in two. We damn near broke all those boys from smoking that spring.

But the trick kinda backfired on me.

We were doctoring for screw worms, and I was riding one of those horses when I rode up on a dirt tank and saw a wormy cow and calf. My horse was kind of an idiot, so I told the feller with me to rope the calf, and I'd rope the cow. I was afraid if I roped the calf, my horse might drag it to death before I could get him stopped.

Well, the feller jerked his rope down and ran out there and roped the calf pretty quick.

The cow took off over the tank dam, and I built to her[15] as hard as I could. When we topped that dam, my horse blew up and went to pitching. Somehow, trying to stay with him, I hit my chest on the saddle horn, and one of those matches struck. That lit all the others.

I can tell you it's not easy to ride a bucking horse while you're trying to hold a burning shirt away from your chest! I should have learned right then and there that payback is a bitch...but I didn't.

Shoot Him Again

Another fine morning, I was doctoring screw worms with the owner of the KCs, Joe Rounsaville. We rode up on a big dirt tank and found

---

15   build to - To ride hard while uncoiling the loop in a rope when chasing an animal.

a cow that had just had a calf, but she had the calf hidden. Joe said that we really did need to find that calf because it would surely have screw worms in its navel.

There was a little white-brush thicket out there about 100 yards, and Joe figured the calf was in that thicket. We were riding real slow through the brush looking for the calf, and Joe jumped a big 10-point mule deer buck.

Joe always packed a .22 semi-automatic pistol in his leggings, and he was riding a big palomino horse named Roman that day.

The deer ran a few yards, stopped, and looked back at us.

Joe pulled out his pistol, stuck it right over Roman's head, and pulled the trigger.

When he shot, did that old horse ever blow up and go to pitching. Every time Roman's front feet would hit the ground, Joe would pull the trigger again.

I guarantee you, I didn't know which way to run or what to do. I finally just bailed off my horse and laid flat on the ground, trying my best to hide behind a foot-tall greasewood bush.

I know that horse made at least 10 jumps because Joe emptied that 10-shot pistol, but he never touched the deer.

Smuggling a Dead Man

When I was pretty young and still working for Joe Rounsaville at the KCs, one day a Mexican feller and I were gathering some horses. We were having to run our horses pretty hard to get around the remuda, and the Mexican's horse took a fall.

When the man hit the ground, he didn't move again. I went over to him, and he was graveyard dead. I was still pretty young, and I knew this feller pretty well.

It sure shook me up, but I went and got Joe. He brought his old station wagon out to where the feller was lying. We loaded him in the back of Joe's car and covered him with his bedroll and some blankets.

The feller lived the other side of the river in Ojinaga, and Joe decided we needed to take him across the border to his house. Joe wanted me to go with him since I spoke Spanish. I was more than a little nervous about taking a dead man across the international border.

It was late at night when Joe drove up to this feller's house. I felt like I was in some kind of a horror movie when we pulled him out the back of that old station wagon.

We laid him out in his bedroll in the front yard, and Joe put a wad of money on his chest, then we covered him up and drove back to Texas.

I didn't sleep a whole hell of a lot for the next few days.

The next morning, I guess his wife found him because I never heard any more about it. For years, Joe sent his wife his pay every month just like he was still working.

You hear a lot about how ranchers mistreated their Mexican help back in those days, but I never saw much of that. We worked hard together every day, and a man was treated with the respect he earned.

Wild Jackasses

Back in the '50s, when the KCs had all those wild horses, they also had about 250 head of wild jackasses. We were in the middle of one of the biggest droughts in history, and they needed to relieve the pressure on what grass they had.

After we'd gathered the wild mares, we went after the jackasses... hell for leather. Joe made a deal with one of those donkey basketball and baseball outfits to buy the jackasses if we could get them gathered.

They'd get the donkeys good and broke, put rubber shoes on them, and take them to churches and high schools. Usually the coaches and teachers would team up against the students and have a baseball or basketball game where they had to ride the donkeys the whole time.

We'd tried penning that bunch of jackasses before, and that didn't work. We knew we were going to have to rope every one of them. You would rope one, and then when someone else caught one, you'd "neck" the two of them together. We tied them neck to neck with pigging strings[16] that had a swivel in the middle, and then we could kinda herd and control them.

We made a drive; and when we'd find a bunch of donkeys, everybody would take off as hard as they could and rope one.

It was wild with everyone roping and trying to get two donkeys necked together with the other donkeys running around on the end of somebody else's rope. Those jackasses would kick, bite, and generally stomp the hell out of you if they got the chance. It got pretty Western.

But the toughest part was when we finally got them to the ranch and had to load them on the trucks. They balked, bit, and kicked every inch of the way. We started loading them at daylight one morning and late that afternoon still weren't finished.

Joe always owned a station wagon, and he finally went and got it. We would run a rope from the donkey, up through the truck, and down to the station wagon. Then we'd holler for Joe to give it the gas and pull that donkey up the loading chute.

Finally, after about 10 hours, we had loaded two trucks full of donkeys.

Love of My Life

After I'd been working for the KCs for a couple of years, one weekend I took off, going to a dance over at the 21 Club in Pecos. On the way, I stopped in Balmorhea for beer and a game of pool and ran into a feller that was home on leave from Korea.

He was trying to get to Ft. Stockton, and I told him I'd take him over there. It was the least I could do with him being one of our soldiers. Well, I took him wherever it was he wanted to go in Stockton and then ran into a friend of mine named Joe Stout.

16 pigging string - A five- to six-foot piece of small rope used to tie animals' feet together, along with a million other things.

Joe said we ought to run down to the Dixie Dog Drive Inn and get a hamburger. He had been dating one of the carhops that worked there, and he introduced me to one of the other girls that worked with her.

I asked this cute little blonde gal to go to the dance in Pecos with me.

She said she wouldn't go to that dance with me, but she'd meet me at a dance there in Ft. Stockton.

I changed my plans pretty quick. Joe and I went to that dance, and I found her, and we danced most of the dances together.

After that when I had a weekend off, I was in Stockton chasing that little gal named Joy.

We were at a movie one night watching *Bus Stop* with Marilyn Monroe, and one of the actors asked the actress if she wanted to get married.

I looked at Joy and said, "What do you think about that?"

She said it sounded like a good idea to her.

So we crossed the border in Del Rio and got married in Acuña 41 days after we met. I had $10, and she had $20. I had just turned 20, and she had just turned 17. Nobody ever thought it would last. We showed 'em different.

After we got married, we moved to the camp at Walker Wells on the KCs. I got Joy hired on as a cook for $50 a month. I was making $150 a month, so we were in pretty high cotton.

The problem was that Joy had no idea how to even make coffee.

We had a Mexican feller there that was the fence builder and windmill man, and he was a pretty good cook. So I got him to help Joy for a few weeks and teach her how to cook for a crew of men.

One night, she told me she sure was tired of beef every meal and asked if we could eat some of the chickens that were running around. So the next morning after I got up to go work, I wrung the necks of several chickens and left them outside on a barrel.

About two in the afternoon we rode in for lunch.

Apache and Joy Adams in the 1950s

Those chickens were still on that table in the hot sun. But now they were about the size of basketballs. All the hands looked at each other, and I went in the house to see what had happened.

I asked Joy if she hadn't seen the chickens that I killed for lunch, and she said, "Oh yeah, I saw them, but they still had their guts and feathers!"

We ate mostly beef after that.

Spilled Milk

I worked on and off for the KCs for almost 10 years. They were awful good to me, but every now and then I'd get the bug to move and work on another ranch for a while, then come back to the KCs.

One time when I had left the ranch, I decided I go talk to Ted Gray about a job on The Kokernot o6 Ranch. I'd hurt my leg and couldn't get one of my boots on, so I went to see him wearing a pair of Indian moccasins.

Ted said he'd heard that I was a pretty good hand and could ride young horses, but he'd never hired a man wearing his house shoes. He hired me anyway, and I worked for him for a while. I sure respected Ted and learned a lot from him.

One afternoon, he showed up with a milk cow and said he was leaving it and for me to milk her mornings and afternoons. One of the reasons I'd left home was because I hated to milk, so I stayed up all night thinking about having to milk another damn cow every day.

Finally, just before daylight, I packed my few belongings in my bedroll and took off. I left Ted the $10 I owed him and a note saying that I appreciated working for him but was moving on.

We're still good friends, and I'd do just about anything for him... except milk a cow.

Fast Gun

After Joy and I had lived on the KCs for a while, she decided she needed some female company, and we moved back to Ft. Stockton. I always had a little bunch of horses I was breaking or someone's horse I was riding for them, but I also got a job in the oil field as a roughneck[17].

Dean Ward and I were roughnecking around Ft. Stockton, and my dad called and told me that a Mexican fellow from the Piedra Azul ranch across the border had a bear that was killing his goats. It was hard to own guns in Mexico, and they needed someone to come hunt the bear.

So Dean and I talked to our boss and got a few days off to help this feller.

We drove down to Dad's River Ranch and got there just at daylight. We could see first light breaking on those mountains over in Mexico, and it sure felt good to be ahorseback again with a friend. We were ready for some open air after working day and night on those oil rigs.

Dad had horses up for us and cups of strong, hot coffee. We scarfed down some hot biscuits with bacon stuffed in them, saddled up, and crossed the river into Mexico. It sure felt good to ride that river again.

We had a deal with the local Mexican authorities that we could kill a deer anytime, as long as we took what meat we didn't need to eat right then to them or a local rancher. Same thing with a bear—you could keep the hide, but you had to give them all the meat.

Ol' Dean and I were riding along that morning and jumped a little four-point buck. I told Dean that buck sure would make good groceries for us, so we shot him and took the back straps and one ham. We hung the rest in a tree. When we ran into the rancher's *vaqueros*, we told them where the meat was.

We rode up a ways and camped for the night.

Neither of us ever took any bedrolls or much in the way of provi-

---

17   roughneck – A slang term for oil field workers.

sions. I never did like to carry a bunch of weight when I was traveling a long way ahorseback.

We'd find a couple of sotol plants pretty close to each other, get them burning, and lay down on our saddle blankets between them. When we'd wake up cold, we'd crawl a ways further and light two more sotols. This would go on all night, and the next morning we might be a hundred yards from where we'd made camp.

We ate venison and tortillas with hot coffee way before daylight the next morning. Then we saddled up and headed back to where we thought the bear might be.

We were trotting along right after daylight, looking for bear sign and enjoying the morning when Dean stopped me and said he saw the biggest buck he'd ever seen in his life. He said since we'd killed the buck the day before, we probably shouldn't kill another one.

I asked him where the deer was, and he said about 75 yards out behind a clump of bear grass. I just eased my horse around to where I could see the deer and jerked my rifle out of the scabbard at the same time I jumped off my horse. I shot the buck and dropped him where he stood.

Dean started cussing me, and 50 years later he's still cussing me for shooting that big buck out from under him.

We went on and made a pretty good circle back in that country and ran onto some more of their *vaqueros* and told them where we'd left the deer hanging. We didn't have any way to carry the horns, so they kept them.

It was the biggest buck I ever killed, but we never did find that bear.

Losing Dad

After I'd roughnecked for about a year, I got a job with a dynamite company. We supplied explosives to seismograph crews around the Ft. Stockton area. We had 17 trucks, and things were pretty busy during that time. I worked my way up to a job where I was in charge of loading the trucks and keeping up with all the paperwork showing where the dynamite was going.

On April 15, 1962, my dad called from the ranch and asked me if I'd come pick him up and take him to Sanderson. He had an ol' boy over there that figured his income tax, and he had to get it done that day and in the mail. So I got a feller to fill in for me and took Dad to Sanderson.

They got his taxes done and in the mail late that afternoon, and we went and ate supper with the feller that did his taxes. We got to my house about 10:00 that night, so he and Mother just stayed with us that night.

Joy had been taking messages for me, and I had several orders for dynamite that had to go out the next morning. So about 1:00 A.M., I drug myself out of bed and went out to the plant to start working on the orders.

About 3:00 A.M., Joy called and said that my dad was real sick, and I'd better come take him to the hospital.

I jumped in the pickup and ran back home. When I got there Dad was sitting on the edge of the bed. He had his britches on and was trying to get his high-top boots on.

I told him to just put on my house shoes, and he grumbled about it. I doubt he'd ever had a pair on in his life.

We got him in the truck, sitting in the middle between my mother and me. It wasn't but about ten blocks to the hospital, and we'd already called the hospital, so they were waiting on us.

We were about a block from the hospital, and my dad said, "I just kinda hated to wake up your mother just because I was feeling bad." Those were his last words. He keeled over in my lap right there.

I rushed to the emergency door and hollered for one of the nurses to bring a stretcher. We got him on it and ran him into the emergency room, but he had had a massive heart attack and was already dead.

My dad and I were really close, and that was one tough night. Some people have to get older to appreciate their parents, but my dad and I were always like good buddies.

He loved to hoorah people, and just about everyone liked him. I still visit him in my dreams sometimes, and it's strange because I'm older now than he was when he died.

After the initial shock was over, I remembered that word traveled real fast in this country. As soon as some of the folks on the other side of the river heard that Dad was dead, they would hit us and take what cattle or horses they could get.

So I called Dean Ward and asked him if he could go down there and watch the ranch until I could get Dad buried and move down there.

Friends like Dean are damn few and far between. He quit his job that morning and headed for the ranch.

Even with him riding ahorseback every day, they stole all of our saddle horses. So I took a leave of absence for a month and moved to the ranch until we could figure out what the family was going to do.

I guess it's just like anywhere else in the world. Most of the Mexicans living across the river from our ranch were good folks and would help you if they could. But the few bad apples sure caused us a heap of grief.

We decided that Joy and I would move to the ranch and run it, and Mother would move to her house in Marathon. My brother David graduated from college the month after Dad died, so he moved to the ranch and took over the candelilla wax[18] operation.

Life on the River

We'd lost our saddle horses, but a feller I knew in Marathon told me he had a couple of unbroken mules, and he'd give me one if I'd break the other one for him. Another friend, Sam Caviness, said he had a big stout mule he'd give me, so I went and picked them all up.

That was a pretty big ol' ranch, and we really needed quite a few horses to take care of it. I heard about a little bunch of horses in Eagle

---

18 candelilla wax – A wax made from the candelilla plant that grows wild in the Big Bend area. The plants were boiled, and the wax extracted. Prior to synthetics, it was used in making chewing gum, floor wax, lip balm, and cosmoline for storing and shipping firearms.

Pass that had come from the 7V ranch in San Miguel, Mexico.

I called the ol' boy that had them, and he said they were unbroke 7- and 8-year-old big stout horses, and he'd sell them to me for $50 apiece. He said they'd been castrated a few years earlier, but then just turned out and they were sure enough pretty rank.

So I went and picked them up. I had a couple of Mexican boys working for me, and Dean was still there, so we started breaking those mules and horses.

One big brown mule we named Alacron, or Scorpion. You'd reach up to put a bridle on him, and that son of a gun would jump and kick you before you knew what hit you. He could sting you with a hind foot from 10 feet away.

He was sure bad to kick, but he was a good mule once you got on him. You could go do anything in the world on him—you could pack a goat, you could rope and tie down cows on him; but when you were getting on or off of him you really had to watch him.

One of the San Miguel horses was kind of a little heavy-set sorrel horse, and we named him Cascabel, or Rattlesnake. He was awful bad to pitch and sure bad to bite you. If you got off while you were working, you needed a long lead rope because he'd catch you not looking and jump and kick or bite you.

Back then, we were doctoring screw worms and riding hard every day, so we finally got that little bunch of horses and mules pretty well broke.

I heard about a feller in Sheffield named Amos Owens that was looking for some horses; so I called him, and he said that he was interested in buying them.

I told him that they were broke but were still pretty rank. He said he had some pretty good boys that he thought could ride them. He offered me $100 a head, so we loaded them up one afternoon and hauled them over to Sheffield and sold them to him.

I was sure glad to get rid of that bunch of outlaws. That was probably about as tough a bunch of little horses as I ever broke.

Back about that time, Jim Delaney and James Ward and I went over to the Pecos 4th of July Rodeo and got in the wild mule race. They had 18 mules for the race and some extras in case they had more entries, so they had about 40 total. There was four nights of the event, and the three of us won it every night.

When the rodeo was over, I made a deal with the feller that owned the mules to buy all of them. So Jim, James Ivey, brother Dave, and I took trucks and trailers up there and loaded all those wild mules and took them to The River Ranch. I hired Jim and Robert Haynes and José Falcon to help me break all those mules.

There were some older, big stout mules that we started first. We tied up four mules each to ride every day.

We'd rocked along there about 30 days riding those mules, and I ran a little ad in the San Angelo paper that I had mules for sale. Some feller from up in Colorado read the ad and called to see about buying the mules.

I told him we had about half of them started, and he asked if we had any sure-enough big rank mules in the bunch. I told him we did, and he said he sure did need them. He said they needed mules to pull cake wagons[19] next year, and they were breaking them to harness cleaning out irrigation ditches and pulling scrapers.

He asked how many I'd sell, and I told him all he wanted. He had a 20-foot gooseneck trailer, and he'd give me $100 a head for all he could haul. He said for me to pick out the biggest, stoutest, rankest ones I had.

I said, "Feller, they'll be in the pen when you get here!"

We got 12 big mules in his 20-foot trailer, and I was never so glad to get rid of a bunch of mules in my life.

Sul Ross Horses

Right before I bought the mules, Sul Ross College wanted to sell 8 or 10 practice horses that their bronc riders used; so I bought them, and

---

19   cake, or cow cake - Also called cattle cubes, cattle feed pressed into small, round cubes.

we had been riding them along with the mules.

One of them was a real good-looking five-year-old dun horse. He'd originally come off of Mr. Cap Yates' ranch, and the dun had bucked a couple of his cowboys off, so Yates sold him to Sul Ross.

Jim Delany started riding the horse, and he pitched pretty hard. But we were riding a lot of rank horses, and Jim got him broke.

Whenever we'd have to make a hard ride up into one of the big canyons to doctor cattle, Jimmy would take that dun horse, so he got good pretty quick. He ended up making a heck of a horse, and I sold him to a calf roper for more than I'd paid for all the horses and mules combined.

Another one of those horses was a little bay horse. He was sure bad to pitch, and I had José Falcon riding him. We were back up in the mountains one day, and that horse blew up and went to pitching. José rode him all the way to the bottom of the canyon.

When he finally got the horse stopped, José told me he'd pulled something loose in his chest and was really hurting. I changed horses with him, and we went on back to the house. José wasn't doing too good, so I took him to the doctor in town. It ended up that he was pulling so hard trying to stay with that horse coming off the mountain, he'd pulled several ribs loose in his back.

That little horse never did quit pitching, so the next year when school started, I just sold him back to the college for a bucking horse. After we got the rest broke, we sold them for $100 a head, so we made $50 each on them.

Boquillas Canyon

It's about 28 miles from the ranch house to the end of Boquillas Canyon upriver. The canyon starts about 10 miles from the house, and I always kept about 100 head of cows up in what we called Boquillas Shut-in. There were big vegas[20] protected by the canyon walls that were solid Bermuda grass, and my cows stayed fat all year

20   vega – A Spanish term for a plain or fertile lowland area; an open area near the river where grass is plentiful.

long up there. It was in Big Bend Park, but nobody really cared back then.

The only problem was that someone had to ride up there a couple of days a week and check on them. When I went, I rode a great big ol' bay horse called Cacahuete (Peanut) for my river horse.

I had to cross the river eleven times to get to the back of the canyon where the river got so tight against the walls the cattle couldn't go any further. If I'd ride back there and couldn't see the cattle, I'd cut for tracks[21] and find them.

On the American side, there was a trail that went up and over the mountain and dropped down into the next vega. It was a pretty bad ol' trail and sure steep to take a horse up. I'd take ol' Cacahuete up that trail and get around the cattle and bring them out.

If the river was on a big rise, I'd have to ride from the house, up Telephone Canyon, into Cow Canyon, and drop off into Marufo Vega, the last vega the cattle could use.

When I went this way, I'd take my tennis shoes with me. After I got there, I'd take my shirt, pants, and boots and roll them up and tie them on the back of my saddle. I was dang sure in the middle of nowhere and didn't have to worry about some pretty gal seeing me in my skivvies.

When I'd come to a crossing, I'd jump off that ol' bay horse and grab him by the tail, and he and I would follow those cattle across the river. Soon as we hit the bank, I'd jump back on him, and we'd drive the cattle down to the next place we had to swim.

He was probably the best river horse I've ever rode or seen. I've been on him when the river was way out of banks, and he knew where every trail went in and out, and he'd head straight for the right place even though you couldn't see the trail.

You might forget a person over the years, but you never forget a good horse.

---

21 cut for tracks - To watch the ground and find tracks left where something has traveled.

Tennis Shoes and a Winchester Rifle

One day José was checking those vegas and found where someone had butchered a cow and tracks leading across the river to the Mexican side.

As soon as he found it, he left the cattle and came back to the house to get me. It was about one o'clock in the afternoon, so we saddled up some fresh horses and about 10 o'clock that night got back to the place where they killed the cow. We spent the night on the river bank and got up early the next morning and found where they'd brought in two or three burros to pack the meat out on.

We could see by the tracks that one of the thieves was wearing tennis shoes; the rest were wearing huaraches[22]. We couldn't follow them all, so we followed the feller with the tennis shoes.

The tracks led straight to the little town of Boquillas and went through a Mexican candelilla wax camp. There was no one in the camp, so we trailed the feller with the tennis shoes right into town.

There was a man named Casus in Boquillas that had worked for my dad and then for me when I took over the ranch. I'd known him all his life. A few months back, his wife was having a hard time with her pregnancy, and we paid to take her to the hospital in Alpine to get medical help to have the baby.

The tracks led right to his house.

He had a brush arbor in front of the house, and he was sitting on a cot under the arbor when we rode up.

I asked him if he'd seen anyone wearing tennis shoes leading a burro loaded with meat come by, and he said he hadn't seen anyone. I was still sitting on my horse, looking straight under his cot, and there was a pair of muddy tennis shoes sitting there.

I told him that I was pretty sure when they butchered that cow, they tied the hide onto a rock and sunk it in a deep hole in the river. I said I knew he was raised swimming in the river and wanted to hire him to come down first thing the next morning to try to find that hide in the water, so I could turn it in to the authorities.

22   huaraches - Mexican sandals.

He said he'd be glad to help.

José and I rode off up to his house in Boquillas to eat supper and spend the night. I told him that I knew this was his town and some of his kinfolks might be involved; so if he didn't want to help me, I understood.

He said that if people didn't have any more respect for his job than that, he wanted to help catch the thieves and see that they were punished.

We were relaxing and soaking up the cool evening breeze in the shade of Jose's house when his wife called us for supper. She had cooked us some big steaks.

We were sitting there enjoying them when José looked at me and said, "This Adams beef sure does taste good, doesn't it?" I told him it sure did.

José's brother was there and told us that Casus had brought in a big load of meat and had shared it with many of the townspeople.

The next morning José and I saddled up early and rode back to Casus' house to get him.

His wife was out tending the cook fire and said he'd left real early that morning. He said to tell me he'd meet us down by the wax camp.

In our leggings' pockets we'd each stashed guns. I'd packed a .357 magnum pistol, and José had a .22 pistol.

When we got close to the wax camp, José said he thought they would have a trap set for us, and we'd be outnumbered. We both agreed that the best thing we could do was to keep our mouths shut under the circumstances.

We rode into the camp, and Casus had a little fire going and had coffee ready and some tacos made. He invited us off our horses.

I noticed a .30-.30 rifle sitting pretty close to his hand.

We stepped off and got some coffee and a taco and just started talking about things besides the stolen cow.

After the sun got up a little bit, an old man came walking off the side of the hill packing an old .30-.40 Craig army rifle, one that would blow a hole the size of a silver dollar through you.

We sat there and visited with him and Casus for a few minutes, and here comes another feller packing a rifle. After about 30 minutes, we had six men that had come off that mountain packing guns that were drinking coffee with us.

Our pistols were looking a little puny about then.

We finally got back on our horses, and they were all standing there looking at us feeling pretty smug.

I looked them over and said in Spanish, "Boys, I'm going to tell you something. I'm not going to push this deal with the cow any further, and I'm not accusing anyone.

"In the future, if y'all get in bad shape and your family is hungry and you need some beef, y'all come to the ranch and tell me.

"We'll come up here together and butcher an old, fat, dry cow[23], and we'll share the meat between us. I don't want to see anybody go hungry.

"But the next time anyone kills a cow without asking, I am going to file charges on them."

We never lost another cow around Boquillas after that.

Oops, Wrong Judge

We always had people who wanted to come to the ranch to fish or just float the river. That's a beautiful stretch of the river with high canyon walls and deep pools. A lot of them would put in their boats at Boquillas and do a two-day float trip through the canyon, then take out at our ranch. Most of them would pay us to gather up all their boats and gear, and we'd haul them back up to where they put in.

One day, a feller named Bob Burleson called and wanted to make a deal with us to pick up his group at the mouth of the canyon and take them back up to Boquillas after their trip. He told me they had an older feller with them, up in his '80s, named Justice Douglas, which

---

23 dry cow - A cow that doesn't have a calf nursing or is not producing milk.

didn't mean anything to me.

Well, I met them at the mouth of the canyon and loaded all their stuff up in the truck. They were all tired and sunburned but had enjoyed a good trip on the river. When we got ready to leave, an old feller and a lady got in my pickup to ride out with me. The old man said he had heard that we were in the wax business.

I told him that we were. I said we had a couple of wax vats to cook it on the ranch but that we also bought a lot of wax coming out of Mexico...which at the time was illegal.

The old feller said, "Just how do you get the wax out of Mexico? If I'm not mistaken, it's illegal to import wax."

I told him, "You can buy all the lawmen in Mexico for $50 apiece. Hell, you can probably even buy the President of Mexico for $100."

Burros loaded with candelilla wax

He said he sure didn't think I could buy the President of Mexico off, and the way he said it sounded like he really meant it.

I got to wondering who the heck this feller was. So I got to asking him if he knew any of the local justices of the peace, like Hallie Stillwell or a couple of others I named.

He said he didn't.

Well, the lady sitting on the other side of him had her arm behind his back and started punching me on the shoulder. I took the hint and shut up.

We got on back to the ranch, and they were all getting in different vehicles for the trip back. The old man got in a car with somebody else, but the lady was still with me. We started down the road, and she said, "Mr. Adams, I hate to tell you this, but that man is not a J.P. He is a Supreme Court Justice of the United States. William O. Douglass."

"Oh," I said, "I guess I see why he didn't think I could buy the Mexican President for $100!"

Not long after my adventure with Judge Douglass, Mother came down and told us she really didn't like living in town and wanted to come back and take over the ranch. She said she'd help me lease another ranch or do whatever I wanted to do.

We looked at a ranch in New Mexico and then one south of Dryden that a feller in Ft. Stockton owned, but nothing looked like anything we could make a living on.

Then a friend of mine told me he had read in *Western Horseman Magazine* about a horseshoeing school in Houston. He said as much as I liked horses and as good as I seemed to be at handling them, I might look into this school.

I called about it, and the lady told me that their school lasted 12 weeks, and that the next class started March 1st. I told her to sign me up and then went down to the ranch and talked to my mother about it.

She said she would help me financially since I wouldn't be able to work for three months while I went to school and because I had been running the ranch for over two years without taking any real wages.

CHAPTER 3

LIFE IN THE BIG CITY

When we moved to Houston in 1964 for me to go to horseshoeing school, I had a pretty tough time driving in that traffic. I was raised in an area where there wasn't even a stop light within 100 miles, much less a freeway. I was scared to death, and probably scared a whole lot of folks in that town with my driving.

The first five days we lived in Houston, I had some kind of a wreck in my truck every single day. I'd back into something or bump somebody in traffic. It was nothing very serious, but I just wasn't used to all those cars and people driving so fast.

One day on the freeway, I cut in front of a feller too quick and hit his front fender. I pulled over and got out of my truck, and he pulled in behind me.

I could tell he was plenty hot when he got out of his car, and he was already cussing me pretty bad.

I just reached over in the back of my pickup and grabbed ahold of my horseshoe rasp. By the time he got to me, I knew he was ready to fight, and he was pretty big; so I just slapped him up the side the head with that rasp, and he dropped like he was shot. He kinda came to and started crawling back to his car. I was afraid he had a gun, so I walked beside him holding that rasp. He said, "Mister, please don't kill me!"

I said, "Feller, if I'd wanted to kill you, I'd have hit you with the edge of this rasp, not the flat side."

He climbed into his car and drove off, and I never heard another word about it.

When we first moved to Houston, we just had a little one-bedroom apartment. The kids slept on pallets on the floor, and we lived pretty close on money.

There was a 7-11 store right across the street from our apartment. One night Joy needed to go over there for something, and the two boys went with her.

We lived on the second floor, and she told me to stand out on the balcony and watch them cross the street. It was pretty dark in front of the apartment building, and she was a little scared. So I watched them cross and then went back inside to study.

In about ten minutes, there was a loud knocking on the door, and my oldest boy was yelling for me. I opened the door, and he said that while they were at the store, a guy came in and robbed it, and the police were looking for him all around the neighborhood. I went over to the store with him and brought Joy and the boys back to the apartment.

That was a lot of excitement for folks who had lived all their lives in the country!

My Kind of School

I didn't have to be at the horseshoeing school until 8 A.M., but I sure didn't want to drive in the morning traffic. So I'd get up about 5:30 and go down, open up the school, and get everything set up for the class.

I made up my mind when I went down there to that school, that I would do everything I could to be the best shoer there. I was the first one there in the morning, and if Bob Gerkin, the owner of the school, had some outside horses to shoe, I'd stay late and help him.

Bob had been a horseshoer in the cavalry at the start of WWII. He learned under a feller named Churchill that made them learn what he called the horse catechism. It was a series of 60 questions that you had to memorize and be able to repeat back to the instructor.

He made us learn it, so I studied that every night when I got home. I'd thought I was a horseshoer when I started that school; but a few weeks with Bob Gerkin, and I realized I'd known about as much as a hog knows about a motorcycle. At the end of the school, I made a hundred on the written test.

Bob said he'd never given anyone a perfect hundred on the shoeing test and gave me a 99. That was the highest overall grade anyone had ever made that graduated from his school. But I worked damn hard to get it.

Bob asked me to stay on at the school as an instructor. He would also get me other horses to shoe when people called the school wanting their horses shod.

Apache and Bob Gerkin taking a break at Bob's horsehoeing school in Houston, 1964

One day, he told me a feller had called and wanted six horses shod at his stables, so I went out and took care of it. When I finished, there wasn't anyone there to pay me, so I left a bill at their barn office.

A week or so went by, and I hadn't gotten paid. We were living pretty tight and sure did need that money.

This feller was a big-time lawyer and had an office in the top of the Humble Building in downtown Houston, so I went up to get my money. His receptionist said he was in a meeting, so I left her another bill and told her I sure needed to get paid.

After another couple of weeks, I still didn't have my check. So I rolled up my bedroll, got my coffee pot and a skillet, and headed for the Humble Building. Folks were looking at me kind of funny when I went up that elevator with my bedroll over my shoulder, holding my pots and pans.

I walked into the reception room of that big law office, and started moving tables and couches and rugs, and laid out my camp. That little receptionist said, "Oh sir, what are you doing?"

"Ma'am," I said, "I came to get my check, and I'm going to camp here until I have my money." I had my check in just a few minutes.

Word kinda got around the horse people in Houston about that, and I never had a problem getting paid again.

I helped Bob for about a year at the school and shoed on the side. I was shoeing for a lot of hunter/jumper stables and shoeing a lot of polo horses.

Finally, I just had too much business, and Bob and I agreed that it was time for me to go out on my own shoeing full-time.

Till You Run Out of Horses or Money

Our local polo club had done real well that year and came within one team of making the national finals in Chicago. They thought their season was over and told me to pull all the shoes off their horses, which I did.

Then something happened to one of the other teams, and our team was in the finals. They called me one night and asked me if I could come out the next day and shoe all of their horses again because they were putting them on a plane for Chicago. Luckily, when I'd pulled off the shoes, if they were still in good shape, I just taped all four shoes together and wrote the name of the horse on it.

They brought in 30 head of horses that morning for me to shoe. I got there at 5 o'clock that morning and brought Joy with me. She'd bring about five head at a time where I was shoeing. When I'd call out a horse's name, she would find his shoes and hang them on a nail in front of the horse.

At about five that afternoon, I put the last set of shoes on the 30th horse. The owner of the team walked up to me and asked me how many horses I could shoe in a day. I told him I could shoe until he ran out of horses or money, whichever came first.

In addition to the polo horses, I did a lot of shoeing for a vet clinic there in Houston.

I was there one day when a lady called the vet and said she needed two mules shod to take on the annual Salt Grass Trail Ride. She said she'd had a couple of different shoers come out, and they had gotten a total of one shoe on the pair of mules. She wanted to know if the vet knew anybody that might be able to shoe them.

Well, I was getting $10 a head back then to shoe a horse. He asked me if I'd do it, and I said I would; but it would be $25 a head, and I didn't want anybody giving me any trouble over what it took for me to get shoes on those mules. The lady said that was fine, to come on.

On the way over there, I told my helper to put the tightest halters we had on those mules and to find something really stout to tie them to.

When we got there, he found a big oak tree with a fork about head high to those mules and tied one to it. I took my rope and slipped the horn knot over the ball of my pickup and then roped one hind foot on that mule. I stepped in the truck and drove until things came tight.

That mule was almost swinging in the air, and I shod that back foot and both front feet while he was stretched out. Then I took the rope off and roped the other hind foot and shod it. We did the same thing with the other one.

Just as we were finishing, that lady came out there and said, "Sir, you sure are hard on mules, aren't you?"

I said, "Yes, ma'am, but neither one of them is hurt, and neither one of us is hurt, and your mules are shod."

The whole thing took about an hour, and I made $50, which was pretty good wages in those days.

Shoeing in the Rain

I was booked up on shoeing for the next several days when one of my good customers from down around Lake Jackson called. There was a hurricane blowing in, and he said they really needed me to come down there early the next morning to shoe a bunch of horses so they could gather all their cattle and try to get them to higher ground before the hurricane hit.

So I called all of the folks I had appointments set with for the next day and told them what was going on. I met the rancher the next morning at about 4 A.M., and my helper and I went to shoeing horses.

As soon as we'd get the shoes on one, a cowboy would saddle him and take off, trying to get those cattle out of the low-lying areas up to higher ground.

It was raining straight down, and the wind was blowing, but we kept on shoeing. We shod around 30 horses that day in about the worse conditions I ever tried to work in. But those folks really appreciated it.

And I got lots of work out of them over the next few years for what we did that day.

CHAPTER 4

BACK TO THE BIG BEND

Home from Houston

In 1972, my mother decided that she was ready to move to town, so I made a deal with her and my brother to move back from Houston and lease the ranch from them.

We had been ranching on a leased place in Dripping Springs while we lived in Houston, and we shipped all our cattle from there to The River Ranch. When we were loading the trucks, one cow jumped out of the pens, and we couldn't ship her.

A few weeks later when we went to Houston to close on the sale of our house, we stopped back by Dripping Springs to try and get that cow. I'd put a set of side boards on my pickup and figured I could get her in the pen with a feed sack and then load her.

It was raining straight down, and I wasn't having any luck getting her in.

Mr. C.A. McCarty, the feller we were leasing from, had a little black horse. He offered her to me if I wanted to try to pen the cow. He had an old saddle that hadn't been ridden in 20 years, so I saddled up and rode off in the pouring rain.

I got the cow up to the pens, but she got smart and took back off for the brush and cedar breaks.

McCarty had an old grass-hemp rope on that saddle that was as stiff as fence wire, but I built a loop and finally got her roped. When I got the rope on her, we were on a little pasture road almost at a crossing where the creek was up and running pretty good.

I shut that little horse down to stop that cow, and that old worn-out cinch just broke like it was made out of straw. That saddle and I both went right over the horse's head and took bridle and reins with us when we went. I just sat there holding on to the saddle, hoping I could stop the cow.

She headed straight up that creek, and I was pretty much water skiing behind her on that saddle.

The horse was plumb loose.

I tried to keep the front end of the saddle pulled up, so it would slide across the water, and the cow finally choked down. I pulled the horn knot off the saddle horn and dallied that rope around a big oak tree and tied it.

I had a nylon rope in my truck, so I went and got the truck and Joy, and we went back to load the cow. I ran that good rope through the side boards and tied one end to a tree. Then I put the loop around the cow's horns.

I just went to backing the truck up. I'd dropped the tailgate onto the bumper of my truck and made kind of a ramp and reeled her in like a fish. We put a come-along[24] between her and the front of the pickup, and I got behind her and coaxed her a little with a hot shot.

We finally got her loaded, but it wasn't too pretty.

It sure pays to have a wife that doesn't mind wallowing all over a wet, muddy cow in the pouring rain. Well, not too much anyway.

We bought a nice home in Ft. Stockton, and Joy and the kids stayed there. I'd come in from The River Ranch or they'd come down every weekend. We did that for about a year, while I was trying to build up my cow herd.

---

24   come-along – A lever and gear device with a cable used to pull heavy objects.

Credit at the Bank

Along about the end of 1972, I heard that the 300-section Pope Ranch was up for lease. A feller named Bishop Bailey had it leased and wanted to sub-lease it; so I went to see him, and we made a deal. I had about 250 paid-for mother cows down on The River Ranch, and I used them for collateral at the bank to borrow enough to buy another 600 head to stock The Pope Ranch.

In 1973, the bottom fell totally out of the cow market. Cows that I owed $400 a head on wouldn't have brought $125 at the sale barn. When I bought those cows, the calves were selling for about 60-65 cents a pound. When my calf crop was ready to sell that year, they would have brought about 19 cents a pound. I was in a bad wreck[25] because that wouldn't even pay the lease and the interest at the bank.

Most folks don't have any idea what ranchers go through. There's days when you feel like you'd be better off just taking your money and going to Vegas. At least the pain would be over quicker.

I never worried about myself; but when you've got a wife, kids, and hired people depending on you, it can sure keep you up at night worrying. I went up and talked to those bankers. They knew I was honest, worked hard, and didn't hang out in beer joints; so they agreed to stick with me. I told them if they would stay with me, I'd stay with the cows, and we'd see if we could all survive it.

My '74 calf crop came in, and they still weren't bringing but about 25 cents a pound. I ran into an old friend that I used to rope steers with, and he said he had a place up in Montana that he needed to stock, and he might buy some of my calves. So he contracted to buy my heifer calves for 32 cents and my steer calves for 34 cents a pound.

We gathered all the cattle into the pens, and I got all the calves stripped off their mommas. I separated the steer calves from the heifers, and then we went through and pulled off all the cull or cut-back calves that maybe had a bad eye, or a lump on their jaw, or were a

---

25   wreck – A cowboy term for a bad situation or an accident with a horse.

little bit crippled and put them in a different pen. We just pretty much straightened up the herd.

He came driving up in the middle of the morning with the trucks boiling up dust behind him. He and I walked through the pens, and he asked how many heifers and how many steers, and I told him.

He asked me what the deal was with the other calves in the back pens, and I told him they were the culls. He asked if I wanted to sell them too, and I said that I sure did.

He said he'd take them too, and I was mighty glad to oblige him. Hell, I would have sold him my dogs, too, if he'd wanted them.

He pretty much saved my life on that deal. I got enough money to satisfy the bank and pay my lease. I was back in business.

Paybacks

While we were on The Pope Ranch, Jim Delaney's little brother Johnny graduated from high school and was looking for a job. He was riding some young horses, so I hired him to come help me.

We were going to gather cattle at first light one spring morning. My boy David and Johnny were always finding something to get into trouble over. I heard them talking behind me but didn't pay much attention.

They'd found a big red racer snake, and Johnny came trotting up behind me and dropped that snake over my neck.

Of course I didn't know what it was and went to fighting and jumping trying to get it off of me. That got my horse spooked, and we nearly had a wreck before I could sling that snake off.

I got on them a little bit, but I didn't say much about it.

But a few days later after a big breakfast of homemade tortillas, eggs, and bacon, we saddled up early to gather a four-section trap we'd been throwing cattle into. We were enjoying the fine morning, and Johnny was riding along beside me on a little sorrel mare that he was breaking. She was still real green.

He was riding with a hackamore, but he didn't have a throat latch on it. The only thing holding it on was the strap behind the horse's ears.

Without any warning, I just reached up and grabbed that hackamore between the mare's ears and pulled it off, so he just had a rein on each side of her neck. For good measure, I slapped her on the butt with my hat, and she went to pitching and then ran off with him.

All he could do was try to hang on.

She kept running and bucking around the pasture until she finally kinda fell in with the cattle. We just penned ol' Johnny with the cattle that morning. I rode up beside him and said, "Payback's a bitch, ain't it, Johnny?"

Not long after that, a friend of Johnny Delaney's gave him a little buckskin dun horse. It was a real good-looking horse but sure bad to pitch. Johnny had him going pretty good and named him Stalin because he was so mean.

It had been raining a lot, and that old country was soaked plumb through. We were trotting down a pasture road and didn't see about a three-foot rattlesnake that had crawled up into a greasewood bush right beside the road.

Johnny was wearing big bat-wing leggings, and that snake struck and stuck its fangs in the wing of those leggings.

Johnny jerked his foot out of the stirrup and was jumping and kicking trying to sling that snake off his leg. That horse blew up and went to pitching for all he was worth.

The boy'd kick at the snake and then try to stay with that horse bucking. He finally got the snake off and got the horse stopped.

It was the wildest ride I ever saw in my life and plenty Western for a while.

Another Damn Milk Cow

One thing you learn if you're going to stay in the cow business—bad times are going to come; and if you're going to stick, you've got to just knuckle down and get tough. After the bottom fell out in 1973, we cut corners every way we could. We sold our home in Ft. Stockton and moved to The Pope Ranch. Joy would drive to town every day to work and to take the kids to school.

One day, she told me she sure wished we had a good milk cow. Well, I left home over having to milk a bunch of cows, and I wasn't about to start doing it again. But I had a boy working for me that said he'd milk the cow if he could have part of the milk, so I gave in.

I had about a four-year-old, Holstein/Brahma-cross cow, and she had a lot more milk than what her calf needed. Valente and I rode out and found this cow and brought her into the pens.

We cut the calf off her and put the mamma cow in a pen, and she was not very happy about it. For the first 15 or 20 mornings, we had to head-and-heel her, and the heeler would step off and milk her while his horse held the heels.

We'd been doing that for about a week when Oscar Cavlin came by the house. Joy told him she wanted to show him her new milk cow, so she took him down to the pen. Our friend said when they got there, the cow started pawing the ground and made a run at them. Oscar looked at Joy and said, "Yeah, that looks like an Adams' milk cow to me!"

Valente decided that since we had a pretty good little garden and a milk cow, we needed some chickens. So I brought some chickens from town, and we fixed up a little chicken house for them right behind my saddle house.

Well, there was a hole in the back of the saddle house just big enough for a chicken to get through. They decided the best place to roost was on my saddle. I'd go out about four or five in the morning to saddle up, and my saddle would be covered with chicken droppings. It didn't take much of that until we started having a lot of fried chicken.

We'd been at The Pope for a little over two years when the feller we sub-leased from had a heart attack and died. The owners decided they didn't want to lease it to anyone anymore and gave me two months to get everything off.

I had about 800 head of mother cows at that time, and we were just coming out of that bad market when we'd lost all our money. Just more fun in the cow business.

I looked everywhere for another ranch to lease, finally gave up, and called for trucks to haul all my cattle to a sale.

We had the cattle penned and ready to load when a friend of mine called and said he heard that The Pack Saddle Ranch was up for lease.

I found out who to talk to and met with them and leased it that night. Then I shipped about half the cattle, the older ones, to the sale barn and the rest to Terlingua to The Pack Saddle Ranch.

Hot damn, we were back in business.

Running Out of Rope

When I was moving off The Pope Ranch, my brother and I bought a little bunch of roping steers, and we went down to gather them. We were going to put on one more team-roping[26] to try and make a little money and then sell those steers, so we wanted to get all 25 of them.

We had about 3 or 4 pigging strings each when we started the drive in that two-section pasture.

Those steers had gotten pretty smart and were good at hiding in the brush. We got about 15 of them penned on the first drive, and the rest got pretty trotty[27] on us. So we went back and rode through the pasture, roping and tying the steers down wherever we'd find them, figuring on coming back and loading them in a trailer.

We used up our pigging strings and our belts, and then used our bridle reins to tie them with.

We had three steers left, and we used our roping ropes to tie two of them with, so we didn't even have a rope to catch the last one with.

---

26 Team-roping - A timed event where two-man teams pay to compete against each other, one roping the head and the other the heels of a steer. Winning teams earn money, as does the producer of the event.
27 trotty - Cattle that tend to be wild, run away from you, and not stay in the herd.

We had to cut some leaves off a yucca and smooth the edges with our pocket knives to make enough of a bridle rein to get back to the truck. It was a couple of miles back to the truck and trailer, and we were trotting along when we ran into the last steer.

David and I discussed it and figured that if we didn't get him right then, he'd sure enough hide, and we'd never find him. So I decided I try to bulldog him. At that time, I'd never stepped off the right-hand side of a horse in my life.

The steer started right down the middle of the road; but every time I'd get up in position and lean over that right side, I'd think better of it. Finally, I got him worn down enough that I was able to jump off the left side of the horse, grab him by the tail, and then grab the horns and bulldog him.

I told David to lope up there and get the trailer, and I just laid there and held that steer until he got back. It took him a while; but he finally got there, and we loaded that steer and then all the ones we'd tied down. That was the first and last steer I ever bulldogged in my life.

Banana Bull

About a week after we gathered those roping steers, we found a big bull we'd missed in the mule pasture, which was about 12 or 14 sections. I knew this was a pretty bad bull, and I called Jim Delaney to come help me gather him.

We drove all day on pasture roads trying to cut that bull's tracks or see some sign of him. Finally, right before dark, Jimmy saw him laying up in some brush.

We jumped our horses out of the trailer and built to him and got him roped. Somewhere in the melee, I got a little too close, and the bull stuck a horn in my horse's chest.

We got the bull loaded in the trailer, but my horse was bleeding pretty bad. We got him back to the house, and Jimmy asked me if I had any bananas.

I went to the house and brought a banana back. Jimmy pealed it and just crammed it into the hole where that horn had been. In less than a week, I was back riding that horse, and he was almost healed.

The next day, Jimmy had to leave; and a boy from Houston named Bill Burton came out to help me. We went over near Maravillas Creek to try and get a little black bull that was running over there. He didn't weigh but about 900 pounds, but he was sure enough mean.

We drove up on a water trough, and that bull was standing there about 200 yards from a mesquite thicket. Bill was driving the truck and didn't have a horse, so I unloaded my horse and broke and ran as hard as I could toward that bull, trying to rope him before he could make the brush. I got him roped just as he got into the edge of the thicket.

He got behind a mesquite tree, and I was trying to work him out on the end of my rope.

I hollered at Bill to bring the truck over and back the trailer up near that thicket. Then I told him to come over and see if he couldn't wave his hat in that bull's face and get him to come out of the brush. I told him I had the bull tied on to the saddle horn, so he wasn't in any danger.

Ol' Bill came over there and swatted that bull in the face with his hat, and the bull came charging out of the brush after him. I was riding a pretty good kind of a horse, so I just kept the rope tight on the bull's neck but let him run behind Bill.

Bill was running as hard as he could, and he jumped right up in the trailer. That little bull went right in after him. Since it was an open top trailer, Bill just went out over the top, jumped in the pickup, and shut the door. He looked out the window of the pickup with his eyes about as big as saucers and said, "Hell, Apache, I thought your rope broke."

I said, "No, Bill. You were doing such a good job loading that bull, I just let him follow you in."

He just shook his head, and I never was sure just how clean his britches were.

Kentucky Fried Adams

Along about that same time, before we sold those steers David and I had gathered, we held a big team-roping.

We started that morning and finished the last round that evening using car lights to light the arena. I had to take all the horn wraps off the steers and feed them, and then unsaddle and feed the horses.

By the time we got through, it was about 10:30, and Joy had already given up and gone home, tired and hungry.

About the time we'd finished all the work, a friend named Bobby Duncan drove up and asked if we wanted a drink of whisky. He came out with a half gallon of Seagrams VO. I took a big slug and passed it around, and we told a few stories and kept taking slugs of whisky, and before long it was gone…and so was I.

Jimmy took me to my house and kinda half-led and half-dragged me to the porch. He knocked on the door and woke Joy up and asked her what she wanted him to do with me. She said something like, "Just pour the sorry so-and-so out in the yard."

Jimmy said it was awful cold in the yard and would it be okay if he put me in the living room in front of the fire. She said it was okay but that I'd better not puke on her floor.

So Jimmy laid me in front of the fire and went back to his truck. He dug around in his truck and found about a week-old Kentucky Fried Chicken bucket and dumped out the half-rotten chicken bones still in it. He brought it in the house and just stuck it down over my head, so I wouldn't puke on the floor.

When I woke up the next morning, I don't know whether I was sicker from the whiskey or the smell of that rotten chicken. I never did drink much, but I had tied one on that night. It was about 10 years before I drank enough to get in any trouble again.

Bad Dreams and Buttermilk

When I leased The Pack Saddle Ranch, I got a little place we called Adobe Walls with it. On the whole place we only had 4 windmills and 5 wells. On top of that, I didn't have enough pipe to even run all the windmills. So the feller that worked for me, Valente, and I would run one mill for a day and fill that tank, then pull the pipe and take it to another mill the next day and run it. It was a heck of a lot of work, but we had to have water.

Between that and taking care of the cattle, we were working about 14 or 15 hours a day. I was still shoeing lots of horses, so sometimes I'd have to leave it with Valente and go shoe all day.

Joy was working for the highway department in Ft. Stockton, and she was staying in town during the week. Once again we were paying the price to stay in the cattle business.

I got in one night about 10 P.M. from shoeing horses on The Chilicote Ranch for Bobby Shelton. I'd shod about 40 head of horses in two days for him and was worn out. Oscar Cavlin was living in a little house near mine on the ranch; and when I pulled in, I saw his light on, so I stopped to visit a minute.

He told me that the night before, a little bunch of wets[28] came walking up and were about to freeze to death, so he let them sleep in my cabin that night. We shot the bull a while, drank some coffee, then I went over to my place to get some sleep.

Nearly every night, and especially if I'm real tired, I have to read a little to relax and go to sleep. There wasn't any electricity in my little cabin, so I had a coal oil light that I used to read by. I lit it and went to bed with my book.

In about 45 minutes, I woke up and was sicker than a dog. I was throwing up and had stomach cramps and thought I was going to die. I smelled something funny and realized that those Mexican boys had put corral cattle spray[29] in my lamp thinking it was kerosene. I'd been laying there for over an hour, breathing that spray while it was burning.

---

28   wets (mojados) - Persons who have crossed the Rio Grande illegally. Not particularly used derogatorily, but to define the difference between those with papers and those without.

29   corral spray – A liquid chemical used on cattle to control flies.

I made it over to Oscar's house, and his wife Zeta said the best thing for me was some buttermilk. She had a milk cow and churned her own butter and had fresh buttermilk. She poured a bunch of that down me, and the next day they took me into Stockton to the doctor.

They ran a bunch of tests on me and said I shouldn't ever be too close to corral spray again because I had about enough of it in my system to last a lifetime.

Anyway, the flies didn't bother me much for a good while after that.

Working cattle at The River Ranch pens

More Crazy Cows

Not long after that little wreck, I ran into Bill and Mary Lynn Johnson over in Marathon. They said they were looking for a place to put about a hundred head of heifers, and I told them that I might have the place. We had worlds of good grass at that time, and I was running about 300 head of mother cows with room for more but no money to buy them.

We made a deal for me to take care of their cattle for them. They delivered them. Not only were they some of the wildest cattle I'd ever seen, they had never been worked horseback. We got them branded; but when we started out into the pasture with them, they just broke and ran like a covey of quail with us trying our best ahorseback to hold them up.

They ran toward the highway and laid the fence down and went right across the road and laid that fence down. Bill and I were riding some pretty good horses, and we were able to jump those downed fences to stay with the herd.

We finally got the leaders turned in about two miles, up on the side of some mountains. We got them back down in some flats and finally got them back onto our place.

I got $6.00 a head a month to take care of those cattle. We kept them for six or eight months, and then the Johnsons sold them.

Another feller wanted me to take care of 1,500 head of steers and offered me $5.00 a head a month, so that really helped Joy and me get back on our feet financially.

I bought some cattle that my brother needed to sell; and with the cattle we'd raised by then, I had about 700 mother cows. The profit off those cows, and what we were running for other people, allowed us to pay the bank off for the money we'd lost when the bottom dropped out of the cow market in 1973.

We'd toughed it out and kept on going. I was sure proud of what we'd been able to do.

Bucking Horses and Arrowheads

When we first moved to The Adobe Walls and Pack Saddle Ranch, our old friend Oscar Cavlin came and talked to me about a job. He had been a good friend of my dad's and had been a paratrooper in WWII, where he had been captured by the Germans. After the war, he came back down to the Big Bend country, and became a river rider[30] in the late '40s.

He had a pension from the government and some retirement from being a sheriff's deputy down in Victoria. He said he'd work for me for a place to live, groceries, and whatever I could pay. I hired him and paid his wife $150 a month plus the house and food, so he wouldn't lose his pension by drawing wages.

He was really good to have on the place because he could do most anything and was a good cowboy. He stayed with me from 1974 till about 1982.

I had made a deal with Jim Delaney on some horses right after Oscar came to work for me, and one day I brought four little 2-year-old horse colts back to the ranch.

Oscar was there when I unloaded them, and he just fell in love with a little red roan colt in the bunch. He asked me if I'd break the colt for him, so it could be his ranch horse, and I said I would. He said he wanted me to take extra care to break him easy and not ever let him pitch.

I started all our young horses, and I told him I'd break this horse any way he wanted me to. So the next day, we went out there and fore-footed him, took him to the ground, and put a saddle and hackamore on him.

Oscar was watching everything real carefully. He said when I got ready to take the horse outside the pen, he wanted to be on his horse leading my horse, so he could keep the colt from ever pitching if he tried to.

So I got on the little horse, and Oscar got on his horse and took

---

30   river rider - After WWII, the government hired men (mostly veterans needing jobs) to ride the Rio Grande and keep diseased cattle from crossing into the U.S.

the lead rope and dallied it up real short so he had control, and we headed out the gate.

We were on top of a pretty good hill, and we rode along it for a couple hundred yards and then started down the other side. About the time we started off the steep side of the hill, Oscar hollered and pitched that lead rope straight up in the air.

When he did, that little horse jumped back and then blew up and pitched all the way to the bottom of the hill.

I got him rode and finally got a hold of the lead rope and got him settled down a little.

When Oscar came riding up, I asked him what in the world happened back on that hill to make him throw that rope and holler like that.

Oscar said, "Oh, Apache, I looked down and saw a perfect arrowhead, and I knew if I didn't grab it then, I'd never find it again."

From then on, I rode his colt the way I wanted to and didn't let him tell me how he wanted it done. He ended up making a real good horse, and Oscar rode him until he left that place.

While Oscar was working for me, the U.S. Customs was sending men to patrol the border and catch dope smugglers. One of these customs men was a big ol' boy that had a hard time walking very much. One morning, he came up and asked me if we had a gentle horse he could buy or rent.

I told him I didn't but that Oscar had a little sorrel horse that would be perfect for him. This horse was gentle and would hang around your camp and just wait for you to feed him every morning. So he went to Oscar, and they made a deal for him to buy the horse.

About two or three months went by, and the agent came by the house one day and told Oscar he really liked the horse but wondered if there was a trick to keeping him fat. He said the horse had lost weight since he bought it, and he didn't know what he was doing wrong.

Oscar said, "Yeah, there is one trick to keeping that horse fat. Every morning you pour those oats in that feed bin, and then in about

2 hours you go back and take all the oats that are still in the feed bin and rub them up and down that horse's back."

The feller thought for a minute and then said, "Oscar, when I go back, there aren't any oats left in that bin."

Oscar said, "That's what I'm trying to tell you. If you feed that horse enough, he'll damn sure get fat."

Pump Jack

During the time I had those 1,500 steers, I had 10 or 12 cowboys working for me in different camps. I had one young boy that went to work for me; and the first time he went out with me to check some cattle, I let him ride a pretty nice horse that I had. Every time I looked up, he had that horse in a lope.

I rode up and told him that the horse was pretty free-going and that he needed to hold him back, not lope him all the time, or he might kill the horse. He said he would, and I sent him off to another area to check some other cattle. When I saw him again, he had that horse in a hard lope.

I had a feller named Domingo working for me. I told him we were going to have to do something to slow that kid down, or he was going to kill some of our ranch horses if he rode them like that all day.

Domingo reminded me we had a big, 3-year-old unbroken bronc that we called Pump Jack because he had this huge head like a pump jack on a well. The next morning about 4:00 A.M., Domingo and I kinda snuck out and roped ol' Pump Jack and put that boy's bridle and saddle on him.

We backed the trailer up to the loading chute and ran him up into the trailer and tied him off. Then we loaded our horses behind him, so he couldn't make a fuss.

Driving up to the area we were going to work that day, I told Bill, one of my good hands, that his job was to stay with that young boy on that bronc. I told him to try and keep the kid out of the fences and the deep draws and if he got bucked off and hurt, to come find us. I said I was going to stop him from loping all my horses to death. Then we went back into the area about 15 miles and unloaded.

The trailer had an open top, and I told the kid that the horse was bad to pitch, and he should get on him in the trailer. When he got on, I just opened that gate and let him go. Bill was already mounted and ready to hang with him.

When we got back to the trailer that afternoon, Billy and the boy were there, and that boy was glued to the back of that horse with both hands on his hackamore reins. I asked Bill how it went.

He said it was a little rough at first, that the horse had pitched and run off for about two miles through the brush and arroyos. But he finally settled down a little and would pretty much stay beside Bill's horse when they trotted around.

I made that boy ride that horse every day until he had him really broke. It sure cured him of that constant loping on my horses. He ended up making a good hand and learned how to take care of his horses.

When we moved over to Adobe Walls, we did a lot of neighbor working[31]. We were over helping Roddy Schoenfield work his cattle, and I'd just bought Joy a big bald-faced horse named Leo. I was riding a big 4-year-old that I was just breaking.

We were riding down a pasture road headed out to make the drive, and my horse started humping up and acting like he wanted to pitch. So I just jabbed him a little with my spurs, and he broke in two. About the third jump, he landed right in the middle of Joy's horse.

Her horse went to pitching and squalling and spinning. Joy got him rode and finally got him stopped. She looked at all of us and said, "I don't know what y'all like about riding a bucking horse. I don't think it's fun at all!"

---

31   neighbor working - Trading work with neighbors rather than paying each other.

Big Gray

When I had all those steers, I always had men hired and was always needing horses. Most folks probably don't realize what it takes to run one of those big spreads.

Depending on the area and how much rain we were lucky enough to get, you might not be able to run over 5 or 10 cows per section. Some of the pastures are 30,000 or 40,000 acres, so you have to make some horse tracks to cover it. We would normally change horses at noon, if we could, and ride a fresh horse in the afternoon.

Somebody told me about a horse sale over in Midland that they were having right before the cow sale, so I went to see what they had. There was a big gray horse that came through. Nobody would bid on him, so I bought him for $340.

I was sitting beside Birch Woodard, and he said, "Oh my goodness, Apache! Did you buy that horse?"

I told him I had, and he said it was his. He'd brought him up here to sell him, so none of his friends would get him. He told me the horse was real bad to pitch, and one of his hands had gotten hung up on him and been drug to death.

I told him I had some pretty good hands at the ranch, and we'd give him a try.

When I got the gray back to the ranch, the boy that I figured on riding him had gotten sick and gone home for a few days to get well. We were starting to work cattle the next morning, so I figured I'd just ride him myself. We had to fore-foot him and almost put him on the ground just to get the bridle on him.

Well, we didn't have room for all the horses in the trailer that morning, so I took one man with me and told the crew to go to a certain spot about 12 miles away. I told them that we'd ride our horses and meet them on the drive.

We hit a trot and loped and trotted those horses across the pasture to meet the rest of the crew. That horse was really nice to ride once you got him saddled and were on his back.

We found the crew and were heading toward them when we came up on a bluff we had to get down. The man with me eased up to the bluff, said it was too steep there, and we needed to move down a little further to go down it.

I eased up to take a look, and my horse stopped about three feet from the edge, so I couldn't see off. I clucked at this horse and kinda pushed him with my legs to get him to take another step to where I could look off that bluff.

When I pushed, that son-of-a-gun took one big jump off that bluff, landed on the slide, and went to the bottom, kinda like that horse in *The Man From Snowy River* movie.

I said to myself, "I think I found me a horse to ride from now on." I kept that horse and rode him until he developed a foot problem when he was about 16.

He was a great ranch horse, and you could take him to the arena and rope steers on him, too. He was one of those special horses that could just do anything.

But he was always bad on the ground. He'd paw or bite you, or jump and kick you in the belly if you weren't careful. You had to give him lots of respect.

I was the only one that rode him until he was about 14, and then I still had to hold him for someone else to get on him. He was perfect once you were mounted, but on the ground he was treacherous.

Hanging Domingo

When we were down at Adobe Walls, my two boys started riding a lot of young horses for people.

Charles Steagall had a little blue roan colt that he wanted us to break, so my son Gary started breaking him. He was a pretty tough horse and would pitch and then cold jaw[32] and run off. My boys Gary and David were only 13 or 14 years old, and they had to go back to school during the week. So I got Domingo to ride this horse a few days to try and get him lined out.

---

32   cold jaw - A horse locks his jaws on the bit and does not respond to it.

We were gathering some cattle one day, and I was cutting out some calves I wanted to ship, and Domingo got on the horse to work on him a little. We had a bunch of cattle gathered up around a windmill, and Domingo was helping hold the herd.

All of a sudden that blue colt just blew up and pitched all around that windmill. He bucked his rider off, right into the windmill.

Domingo's head went through one of those angled cross ties, and he was hanging by his neck. I think ol' Domingo's neck was about three inches longer when we got him down off that windmill. We had to take him into the doctor, and they said he was damn lucky to be alive.

This ol' cowboy life isn't always as romantic as it's made up to be.

Flying High

When I had all those steers pastured for that feller, he came down to check his cows with a Super Cub airplane.

He took me up, and I thought that was pretty neat, so I decided I needed to learn how to fly. He told me he was an instructor, and he could teach me how to fly while we were checking the cattle. So I got in a few hours of instruction time with him over the next few days.

The next time I went into Ft. Stockton, I went out to the airport to see how much airplanes cost. I was talking to Bill Harget, and he said he had a 172 with low hours that was in real good shape. He made me a deal, and I bought that airplane.

Over the next few days, I took more lessons there at the airport. Then a friend I knew that was a pilot came up, and we flew the plane back to the ranch. I had about 7 or 8 hours by then.

We were flying over a pretty good dirt road on the ranch, and he told me to put the plane down on it. When we got on the ground, he got out and told me to take off and make a circle and land again by myself.

So I took off and got about 100 feet off the ground and looked down and thought, "Adams, what in the hell are you doing up here in this airplane by yourself?" That's a pretty scary feeling the first time you solo, I don't care how tough you think you are.

I landed, and he came up to the plane and told me to take off again and do a series of touch-and-go take offs and landings. So for about an hour I did that. After that, I just went to flying when I wanted to.

I had about 200 hours, and one day I flew into the Ft. Stockton airport for fuel.

Bill Harget came up to me and said, "Apache, you really need to get your license before you get us both in trouble."

I told him I already had my medical and had passed all of my written tests, I just needed a final check ride.

He said okay, but that he was just too busy that day to go with me on a check ride.

For several more months, I tried to get him to give me the check ride; but we never could get together, and he was always too busy to go with me.

One day I'd been helping Jim Delaney work cattle and had my bedroll and saddle in the back of my plane. Since I needed fuel before I went back home, I flew into Stockton to fill up. And I figured I'd just pull one on old Bill and maybe get him to give me that check ride.

I landed and taxied up by his little shed, got out, and went in with my bedroll over my shoulder. I threw that old dirty bedroll down on the floor and told his wife that I wasn't leaving until I got my check ride.

She went and got Bill, and we all had a big laugh.

But I got my check ride.

Full of Bull

My brother David sold a ranch he owned over in Jeff Davis County that bordered the Boy Scout Ranch. He had a real nice set of about

250 crossbred cows.

He didn't want to sell them, so he asked me if I'd pasture them for him. In the bunch was an old Brahma bull that was pretty bad about fighting. After I'd had them a while, I made a deal to buy them from him.

I had a couple of fellers come down and help me bring the cattle to the pens, so I could put my brand on them. I told them that if we ran onto that bull and he gave us trouble, just to leave him, I'd come back and take care of him later.

We had a bunch of cattle headed to the pens, and Roddy Schoenfield came riding up to me and said he saw that bull brushed up in a little clump of cedar.

Well, I hadn't told those boys helping me what kind of a bull he was, just that there was one bull in the bunch that was pretty bad.

He and I rode over there, and I saw that the bull in the brush was an old longhorn bull that we'd used for years in the roping arena. He was as gentle as a dog, but I saw a good opportunity to hoorah old Roddy a little.

I told him to back me up, but I didn't want to get anybody else hurt. I took my rope off my saddle and jumped off my horse and went into that thicket with the bull.

Roddy was telling me how crazy I was the whole time.

I just walked up to that bull and dropped my loop over his head and led him out of the brush.

Roddy couldn't believe it.

Then I got back on my horse and led the bull over to the herd, reached down, and just pulled my rope off of him.

I looked at Roddy and told him, "You just have to know how to handle a bad bull."

Gary

Jim Delaney bought about 20 head of unbroke mules one time, and was planning on breaking them and selling them. About that time, mules got kinda popular, and people were having mule races and ropings using mules. He thought he could make a little money selling them.

My youngest boy Gary was a pretty good little bronc rider, and he and some of his friends each took a mule to break. He had his mule started and brought him down to the ranch one day when we were gathering cattle.

I saw a bunch of cattle way up on top of a pretty rough mountain, so I told Gary to take his little mule and work his way up there and bring those cattle down.

He got to the top, and when he started hollering and slapping his leggings trying to get those cattle off the top of the mountain, that little mule broke in two and went to pitching off the side of that steep mountain. I mean, he was bucking and bawling and squealing and really flying down that slope.

Oscar Cavlin was with me and said, "Apache, there's no way that mule can stay on his feet down that mountain the way he's bucking."

I said, "Hell, Oscar, he's a mule. He'll still be standing when he hits the bottom."

Gary got him rode and had a big ol' grin on his face when we rode up to him. He said, "Boy! That was a heck of a ride off that mountain, Dad!"

Of course, I was as proud of him as I could be, the way he rode that mule. But I didn't let on to that and told him it sure was a ride; but the problem was that the cattle didn't come with him. He was going to have to do it all over again.

He looked up at them, said, "Oh yeah," and rode right back up there and got the cattle.

Later on, Gary was working for The Yarborough Ranch and breaking a lot of young horses.

One day, I was driving down the rode toward Alpine and saw him riding one horse and leading another one down the bar ditch toward town. I stopped and asked him what he was doing.

He said he was out of snuff and just thought he'd ride one bronc to town, which was 20 miles away, and lead the other one. Then he planned to change horses and go back to the ranch.

I told him to lope on up about a half-mile to a little roadside park and tie the horses to a tree, and I'd take him into town.

We went in and got his snuff, but I never understood how a feller could want a dip of snuff bad enough to ride 40 miles on two green broncs to get it.

One day, I got word at the ranch that Gary had been in a real bad car wreck in Ft. Stockton. By the time I got to town, he was already gone.

There's no way to describe to someone what it's like losing one of your kids. You have to go on with life, but you sure don't ever get over it.

He's buried out at the cemetery in Stockton, and sometimes I just go by and have a talk with him. I don't know if he can hear me or not, but it usually does me some good anyway.

CHAPTER **5**

INTO THE '80s AND BEYOND

Big Bucks in the Fur Business

Along in the mid-eighties, my brother got pretty big in the fur-buying business. He got me involved, and I would buy furs from trappers around the area where we lived.

I had a feller working for me who was real good at washing and cleaning up the furs after we'd buy them, so that brought us a little more than the average price for our furs.

That first year, I made pretty good money in the fur business, so the next year I decided I'd take my airplane and expand my territory.

There'd be a rancher that would call me and say he had maybe 50 or 60 ringtails, 30 to 40 bobcats, a few coyotes, and lots of fox. I'd just fly over to his ranch and buy them on the spot. I got to where I'd fly to all the little surrounding towns. Folks would meet me at the airport on certain days, and I'd buy their furs. We bought a lot of furs for several years and made good money out of it.

By that time, my brother had gotten completely out of the business, so everyone was selling to me. I talked to the people in Seattle, Washington, that I was shipping my furs to, and they said the market was really strong. They told me to buy everything I could get my hands on and that I dang near couldn't pay too much for them because they were moving so well.

So I made a deal with the bank, and we were buying $30,000—

$40,000 worth of furs a week and shipping them to Seattle. I was scared to death, but the buyers up there said to keep sending them. I had a crew of men that worked full-time just cleaning, brushing, and packing furs. We would get a trailer load, and I'd take them to the airport in Midland and ship them to Seattle.

We had been warehousing them with the Seattle Fur Exchange and had over 100,000 furs that we were going to sell at this big sale coming up. Joy and I got on a plane and headed for Seattle, and I told her we were about to MAKE our first million.

We got up there and our fox, ringtail, and bobcats all sold. But not one coyote pelt sold. I had about $20 apiece in over 30,000 coyote hides, and we finally got $1.50 each from some company that made fishing flies. On the way home, I told Joy that we'd just LOST our first million.

She's often said, "Being married to you hasn't been all fun, but it's damn sure been exciting!"

Closed Range

In the mid-eighties, Brewster County passed a law that said instead of people having to fence out other folks' cattle to keep them off their land, the cattle owners had to fence in the cattle they owned to keep them inside their own property.

There were lots of us, especially down in that Terlingua country, that had always let our cattle run wherever there wasn't a fence to stop them. The new law put an end to that.

I went to gathering and straightening up my herd and selling the older cows. I ended up with about 150 head that I could take care of on my ranch. Before the law changed, I always had 8-10 men working for me and 25-30 horses. With the smaller herd, I got down to one hired man and needed to sell some horses.

I called a friend of mine, Bill Madden, who was a real good horse trader. I had bought lots of horses off him, and he helped me sell my extra horses. I started going to some horse sales with him, and he taught me some of the things that make a horse work better in the sale ring, how to really show a horse off and make him bring top dollar.

I was making a little off my smaller cow herd. I was riding some young horses for people, and Bill helped me make more off of the horses I was selling.

Joy had bought an abstract and title company in Alpine, and she was trying to get that business going.

The horse trading business was something that I really enjoyed, and I've continued to do that the rest of my life. If I'm selling a horse to an individual, I always try to tell them everything I know about the horse. Happy customers will bring you lots of business and recommendations to their friends.

I was keeping some 2- and 3-year-old colts at the ranch, and I had a man named Clay Webb that had stayed on to help me with the cattle. There were some folks in town that wanted to look at my colts to buy. So I went down to the ranch, and Clay and I went out to gather the horses.

They were all bunched up around one of the dirt tanks, and we got them started back to the pens. I told Clay to ride on ahead and take the truck and trailer back to the pens.

I was riding a big, nice sorrel horse that I'd just traded for. The colts broke into a long lope headed in the right direction, so I just stayed out beside them on my horse.

We started down in a little draw, and my horse was watching the colts instead of where he was going. He stepped into a big hole that was covered with grass, and we turned the damnedest chili flip you ever saw. I landed on my head and shoulder. It almost knocked me out, and I knew I was hurt.

Luckily, we were pretty close to the pens, and Clay saw the whole thing happen. He jumped on his horse and came back and caught my horse and brought him to me. I told him I couldn't ride, but I thought I could lead my horse to the trailer if he could get the colts in the pens.

I got into the truck, and I'd drive a little ways and then stop and lay down in the seat. I was sick to my stomach, and my shoulder was sure hurting.

When I got to the main road, I stopped one of my neighbors in his truck and asked him to go down to Oscar Cavlin's house and tell him that I was hurt and needed some help. Oscar took me into town to the hospital where they told me my shoulder was dislocated and my collar bone was broken.

After I'd healed up pretty good from that wreck, I decided I'd enter a roping up at Sul Ross College. I was riding a young horse that hadn't been roped on much, but I wanted to see how he would do. Before the roping started, the rodeo coach at the college rode over to me and said they had a boy that was going to try out a new bucking horse mare, and he wanted me to be the pick-up man for the kid.

That horse sure did pitch; but the boy got her rode, and I ran in to pick him up off the horse. When I got there, the horse pitched right into my horse's front legs, and both horses and the kid ended up on top of me.

This time it didn't dislocate my shoulder—it broke it all to pieces. So I spent most of the next three months in a recliner chair. I didn't think I'd ever get over that wreck.

Ray Hunt

I always said there were only two things a cow was good for: one was to eat, and the other was to train a horse with. I grew up ahorseback and always loved training and working with young horses. The men that taught me were good hands with a horse, and they used the methods they had been taught, which weren't always easy on the horse.

Sometime along in the mid- to late 1980s, I heard about a feller named Ray Hunt who was supposed to be the very best at training horses. This was before the term "horse whisperer" came into use.

Ray used more gentle techniques in his training than the folks I'd been around. I heard he was really good from some top hands that

I respected, so I decided I'd see what it was all about. I went to one of Ray's clinics and immediately knew that this feller was something special.

There were a lot of things that he taught that I didn't realize I already knew. Like always knowing where your horse's feet are, which one was about to leave the ground, and which one was about to hit the ground.

There were a lot of things I didn't know, and I was sure eager to learn them from Ray. I knew I could get a horse to do anything he was physically capable of doing. I could MAKE him do it, but Ray showed me how to make him WANT to do it. He showed me how to make the right thing easy for the horse and the wrong thing difficult.

A horse doesn't respond so much to pressure as he does from the release of pressure. Way too many people get a horse to doing something they want, and instead of rewarding him with the release, they just put more pressure on the horse. Then he really doesn't know what you want.

Now, I won't tell you that I don't revert back every now and then and get after an old horse pretty good.

I've always bought horses nobody else wanted or maybe couldn't handle, and sometimes you have to get a horse's attention pretty quick to keep somebody from getting hurt.

But I don't ever hold a grudge with a horse, and I try to always give them an even break. I can probably get more sentimental about some of the horses I've owned than I can about some of the people I've known.

Catch 22

We had a little bunch of wild cows that liked to hang out around Terlingua Creek. They got pretty trotty and would hide whenever we were gathering the other cattle.

One day, Joy and I were riding around the ranch in the pickup looking at the cattle and ran up on a bunch of them. There was one

3-year-old maverick bull in with them that was kinda the ring leader of the group. I thought if I could get him caught, the rest of them wouldn't be so hard to handle.

I had a horse named Mr. Big in the trailer with us, and he could be pretty treacherous. Joy was riding a big gray team-roping horse of mine. When we unloaded the horses, those cattle broke and ran, but I jumped on ol' Big and roped the bull.

I'd roped him around the horns instead of the neck, and I couldn't choke him down. He just kept turning to face me, and I couldn't get him to step over the rope, so I could trip him. I messed with him for about 30 minutes and never could get him down.

So I told Joy I was going to take my rope off my saddle horn and grab another rope and try to catch him around the neck. And I told her to stay about 50 yards in front of the bull to hold him up, but to be careful because if she had to push ol' Gray and really get after him, he'd probably blow up and pitch with her.

That didn't make her very happy at all. She wanted to know the breaking point between "sorta running" and "wide open." I told her she'd know when Gray started pitching.

Then I went over and got the other rope and got the bull roped around the neck, tied down, and finally loaded in the trailer.

The next time we worked that area, we got those other cattle gathered, but Joy never was very happy with me about the situation I had put her in that time on ol' Gray.

Roping a Mountain Lion

I'd put together a pretty good bunch of hounds about that time, and we had to exercise the dogs on a regular basis. One morning, we were letting the dogs run a little. Domingo and another feller were riding some young horses, and I was riding a young mule I was breaking.

We were checking a water line and rode up to the foot of Adobe Walls Mountain when the dogs opened up and started chasing something. I thought they were after a fox or a coon; but in a minute my oldest dog, ol' Troubles, started baying. I told those boys that Troubles was pretty true, and we had us a cat of some kind.

We followed the dogs up into a big rock slide, and they had about a 70- to 80-pound female mountain lion treed on a big rock. The dogs had her surrounded, but none of us had any kind of a gun. So I jerked my rope down and just kinda pitched it at the lion on that rock. She swatted at the rope, and I pulled it up tight around her front paw.

That mule was pretty green and, when the cat started throwing a fit with the rope on her paw, decided to take off.

We jerked the lion off the rock, and then the dogs all jumped on the lion. So I was dragging a lion around in circles with my mule and with a bunch of dogs chewing on the cat, and she was putting up a pretty good fight with three legs.

I finally got the mule stopped, and Domingo and the other feller jumped down and got the dogs pulled off the lion. Domingo finally got another rope on her hind foot, and we stretched her out.

The other boy got the dogs tied off to a persimmon tree, and things kinda settled down. I sent the feller back to get the pickup; we had a dog cage in it. We got a forked limb and kinda kept the lion's head between the forks until we got her into the cage and got it shut.

We took her to the JA Campground, a little place Joy and I owned. We kept her in a cage there for about a year. Ever so often, I'd take a pair of horse hoof nippers and a pigging string and get her to reaching out of the cage with her paw. I'd snag it with the pigging string and trim her claws that way. Finally, a feller came by and bought her from us.

Teaching a Horse to Fly—Almost

We were neighbor working for Brian Larremore in the mountains down south of Alpine one day and had a bunch of cattle coming off the side of a pretty steep mountain. All of a sudden they started to turn off in the wrong direction. My son David and I saw what was happening and bailed off the mountain in a dead run, trying to turn those cattle before they could get too far.

One ol' brown tiger-stripped cow and her calf had been pretty trotty all day, and they broke and ran ahead of the others. My horse was running all out trying to head her and jumped some bushes on the side of the mountain.

Behind the bushes was about an 8-foot drop off. We landed in a pile with the horse on top, and my leg was broken in ten places from the knee down. My spur had hung on something during the fall, and the force tore my Achilles tendon in half.

Some of the other men saw what happened and came riding over to check on me. One of the men was riding a double saddle blanket, so he jerked one of them off his horse, splinted my leg in it, and tied it with pigging strings.

When my son got to me, he told me I was lying in a big ant den.

I said, "You leave me and these ants alone. I've got one move in me, and that's when y'all get me out of here. In the meantime, I'll handle the ants."

I was hurting bad and knew I was really messed up. At times like that your mind comes up with all sorts of things: *How long is it going to take this mess to heal? Will I ever be able to ride again? Hell, are they going to have to take my leg off?*

They went and got a 4-wheel-drive Suburban and had to build a make-shift road off an old ranch road to get to me. That took several hours, and we didn't have so much as an aspirin for the pain. Eventually, they brought an old mattress, rolled me up on that, and loaded me.

When they moved me, there was a pretty good little pile of dead ants left behind that I had been killing one at a time.

I was hurting so bad that I got Luther Anderson, who was driving, to stop and cut me a mesquite limb to put between my teeth. I had been gritting them so hard, I could feel them chipping. We made it almost to the main highway before I had that limb chewed up and he had to stop and get me another one.

They finally got me into the emergency room in Alpine.

Dr. Pearce took one look and said there was no way they could do anything with me there. He said I'd have to go to the hospital in Odessa, where they operated on me that night.

The next morning, the doctor came in, looked at my leg, said it looked good, and that I had to get up on a walker and walk down the hall.

They had one of those little triangle deals over my bed, so I grabbed it to pull myself up. But my other leg didn't want to move, and I told the doctor.

He threw my hospital gown back and looked at my good leg. He said, "My gosh! What happened to this leg? It looks like you've got the chicken pox."

I had those ant bites all over it, and the knee was swollen and messed up from the fall.

He said he'd probably have to operate on that knee when my other leg had healed. But I never have had that done. They told me that I'd be able to walk pretty well again, but that I probably would never be able to ride a horse again.

After I got home from the hospital, there were some times when I'd just get in my truck and drive around at night trying to get my mind off the pain when I couldn't sleep.

Once I was pretty much healed up, the leg was still giving me fits and just didn't feel right. The doctors said everything was put back together right, and I'd just have to let time finish healing me.

One day, I went with Dean Ward and Jim Delaney out to look at some cattle, and we were pulling a trailer. On the way back, something got wrapped around the axle of the trailer, and we had to stop and try to get it off. I crawled up under the trailer to help but then was having a hard time getting back out because of my leg.

I hollered at Jimmy to help me get out. Without even thinking, he just reached down and grabbed my bad leg and drug me out from under the trailer.

You talk about seeing the stars, the Milky Way, and the Northern Lights all at once! I did.

When I finally got my breath back, they got me into the truck, and the pain went away. Back at the house, I stepped out of the truck real easy, not knowing if my leg would hold or not. There wasn't any pain, and I could walk almost as good as before I broke my leg. I never had problems with the leg after that, and I've ridden many a mile and roped a lot of cattle since then.

Old Delaney said I should have paid him all that money instead of the dang doctors.

Making New Cowboys

When my grandson Dusty was about a-year-and-a-half old, he came to live with Joy and me full-time. Joy was really busy with her title business, so Dusty started going everywhere with me. He was horseback from the time he was about two.

I could see real quick that he sure needed to be potty trained because packing diapers and changing them while working cattle wasn't working too good. When he was old enough to understand what I was telling him, I told him he had to let me know when he needed to go to the bathroom.

If he'd mess in his pants, I'd just take them off, find a cold water trough, and dunk his little butt in that cold water to clean him up. It didn't take long before he'd tell Grandpa when he needed to go. That's probably not how child experts would tell you to potty train a kid, but it dang sure worked.

When he started teething, I'd just let him ride in my lap in the pickup, and he'd chew on the steering wheel. That seemed to make his gums feel better, so that's the way we handled that deal.

I found a horse the customs people had confiscated from some drug dealers who had been packing marijuana across the border with him. He was as gentle as a dog, and you couldn't do anything to excite him.

Jim Delaney loaned me a little kid saddle, so I put Dusty on that horse, took the saddle strings and just kinda tied him up there. We'd take off and check cattle with ol' Dusty right behind me on his little horse with me leading him.

If I had to ride off in a long trot or a lope and look at some cattle, I'd tie Dusty's horse to a tree and tell him to sit there and wait. I'd tell him that I'd be right back and he'd be just fine. He knew when I told him to stay somewhere, that was what he was supposed to do. He knew I would always come back and get him.

When Dusty was about 3, we were gathering a bunch of cattle, and a friend of mine named John Duerkop was with us. Dusty and I were riding the ridge line, John was a little below us, and some other men were working the brush down in the bottoms. There was a bunch of cattle brushed up down there, and the fellers were having trouble getting them out.

I told Dusty to stay right there on top, and I'd go help the other men and then come back up and get him. On the way down, I ran into John. I told him to just get Dusty and for them to ride on over to the next ridge and stop the cattle if they tried come out behind us, and we'd meet them there.

We finally got those cattle out of the brush and started up the trail. I could see John sitting on his horse by himself where I told him to meet us.

He rode down and met me and said he'd tried every way in the world to get Dusty to come with him. But Dusty told him that Grandpa said to stay right there until he came back, and Dusty wasn't moving.

When I got to him, ol' Dusty was kinda worried that I might be mad at him. He said, "Grandpa, John wanted me to go with him. But you said to stay here till you came back, and that's what I'm doing."

I've never been prouder of him, and I told him so. It sure made me feel better about leaving him alone ahorseback.

Grandson Dusty ahorseback at age 4-1/2

From Stockbroker to Cowboy

John Duerkop had been a successful stock broker for years in Chicago and decided he'd had all he wanted of that life. He moved to Alpine around 1990 or '91. John had met Joy because she took care of the title work on his house when he bought it.

During the closing, Joy mentioned that when she finished, she needed to get down to the ranch and help her husband work cattle. That was when I had my leg in a cast from that horse wreck and was on crutches.

John told Joy that he would really like to go with her and was willing to help in any way he could. Joy said we could use all the help we could get and for him to come on.

When they got there, I had men out gathering the cattle and had a horse saddled and waiting for Joy. We saddled up another horse for John and took off to get the cattle in.

After we got the cattle penned, we went to the house to eat a late lunch, and I started visiting with John. He'd been a pilot in Vietnam and won the Distinguished Flying Cross. He was a true hero in my book.

He told me he had retired and still played the market a little on his computer, but he really wanted to learn to be a cowboy. He said he'd work for nothing if I'd teach him.

Well, Joy had started trying to trade in the stock market and had bought some heating oil futures and lost all her investment in about 30 days. So I told John I'd make him a deal. I'd try to make a cowboy out of him if he'd teach Joy how not to lose money in the stock market.

He said that sounded like a deal to him and reached out, and we shook on it. Then he turned around to Joy and said, "The way not to lose money in the stock market is to stay out of it." Then he turned to me and said, "All right, I've done my part. When do we start cowboying?"

John ended up being a great friend and worked lots of cattle with us. He always did exactly what he was told and ended up being a good hand that we always liked to have along.

He got cancer and sure fought it hard. It was hard to watch him go through what he did with all the chemo and radiation. True to his nature, though, he never complained and always said he was going to beat it and get ahorseback again. We lost him in 2008, and I sure do miss having him around.

Mad Cow

That same day that John first came down and helped us, my son David was helping work cattle, too. I was driving behind the herd in the pickup, trying to keep up and see what was going on, and I saw Joy ride over and try to get a cow out of the brush.

Well, this was an old high-horned cow with a baby calf. I knew the mama was meaner than a one-eyed polecat, and I yelled at Joy to back off from her before that cow hooked her horse. She did, and in a minute David rode up to see what was going on.

I told him to go try to work that cow into the herd but to watch her because she was sure enough mean. He said she wouldn't bother him and rode over and got too close to her.

Sure enough, she ran at him. Before he could get his horse turned, she ducked her head under his horse's belly and flipped horse and rider upside down.

David got up and was trying to run for cover, but the sole of one of his boots had come loose at the toe and was just hanging on at the heel. So when he ran, he had to sling that flopping boot sole every time he took a step.

Santos, one of my men, saw what was happening and ran his horse over and started slapping that cow in the face with his rope. She started fighting him, and David finally got his horse back and got mounted.

That could have turned out to be a bad wreck if Santos hadn't been thinking pretty fast.

Pushing on the Reins

One morning, my brother David called me and asked if I might bring a couple of men and help him gather the wild jackasses off our old River Ranch. That was rough country with some dang steep mountains and lots of gullies and washouts.

Back in the candelilla wax days, the men gathering wax had used burros to pack the wax plants on, and lots of those burros had been turned loose on the ranch. They had multiplied to where my brother had about 250 wild burros running on the ranch, eating grass he couldn't afford to lose.

I took several fellers down there, and David had gotten a few boys. We had 12 or 14 men all together and gathered about 50 head.

David was going to ship them to El Paso to a horse sale.

I got to talking to him and Lee Roberts, who was running the ranch for him, and I told them I had an idea. "Those burros probably wouldn't bring more than $25 or $30 each at the sale. Why don't you take them up to Marathon and put on a donkey team-roping? You'll probably make more than you would selling them."

They did it and had about 300 teams show up to rope donkeys. That was a money-maker!

David decided that was a pretty good deal, so he only sold the older jacks and kept the younger ones and the jennies and turned them back out on the ranch.

Remuda in The River Ranch pens during the
Wild Burro Gathering, mid-1990s.
Notice "Car Mountain" in the background.

Apache winning the buckle at
The Wild Burro Gathering at The River Ranch, mid-1990s

Every year after that for about 15 years, we would have a big gathering on a weekend. About 45 or 50 cowboys would show up to help gather the burros on the ranch.

On a Saturday morning, we would all work together to try and make a drive on those donkeys and pen the ones we could. Donkeys don't pen like cattle. They will get close to the pens and then turn back and flat run over you.

As soon as we had penned what we could, it was every man for himself roping and tying burros. We had some boys that just liked to ride around and drink beer. They would pull a big trailer and pick up burros the ropers had tied to bushes all over the ranch.

The man who had the most donkeys roped and tied by Sunday afternoon won a nice buckle. That became one of the most prestigious buckles in our part of the country because it was pretty tough roping those donkeys up in the mountains that they'd lived in all their lives. It wasn't an event for the fainthearted, and I still don't know how we kept from getting somebody killed.

Over all the years we had that gathering, I won the buckle all but two years. I had a big advantage in being raised on that old ranch and knowing every rock and trail on it.

But then I didn't have much pull-up in me either, and I'd never slow down till I had one roped. I told one feller after he and I had a pretty good horse race after a donkey and I roped it, "You can't ever pull on those reins. You've got to keep pushing on them."

Rope-off for the burro-gathering buckle.
Apache is second from the left; he won the buckle.

The weekend after we gathered the burros, we would take them to Marathon or Ft. Stockton and have either a team-roping or a ranch rodeo. The rodeos were sure fun to watch because those donkeys don't act like cows and might go any direction or do anything you don't expect.

We'd have a wild jenny milking as one of the events. The milker would have to stick his head down by that jenny's flank and try to get some milk out of her while two of his teammates tried to hold her. The two guys doing the holding had their legs tied together to make it a little more exciting.

David finally decided he'd sell all the donkeys off, so for a couple of years we would gather them, and he'd take them to the sale. That was sure a lot of fun, and we got lots of good riding and roping, and quite a bit of whiskey drunk and stories told around the campfire.

Pinto Canyon

One night in 1994, I got a call from a feller I knew who said he had moved all his cattle off of The Pinto Canyon Ranch down below Marfa, all but about 30 head that they couldn't gather. That's a real rough old ranch, and it's pretty tough to work. He offered to go halves with me on all of the remnants that I could gather for him.

I took a couple of boys over there, and it took us three days; but we gathered all of his cattle. We never penned a cow. Every one had to be roped and tied down and then loaded in a trailer.

Dogie Delaney, Jimmy's son, was helping me.

One day, he was riding a little paint horse that I had bought from Fayette Yates. The little horse didn't weigh 900 pounds, but he was all heart.

Dogie and another hand named Juan jumped two bulls out of the brush and chased them up onto a pasture road. The bulls were running right down the road, and Dogie yelled at Juan that he would rope the one on the right and for Juan to take the one on the left.

Dogie threw first, and his loop went right around the bull's right-hand horn, and the bull on the left stepped into the curl of Dogie's loop. He had both of them on the end of one rope. He was tied on hard and fast, so he just shut that little paint down and jerked both those bulls to the ground. He and Juan jumped off and tied them down.

When we took them to the sale, those two bulls weighed a total of 2,300 pounds. That was one tough little horse.

When we finished, I told the feller that owned the cows that I sure would like to lease that ranch if the owners wanted somebody else on it. He got me in touch with them, and we made a deal on the phone for me to lease the ranch. Before I moved my cattle onto the place, I was riding all the outside fences and making sure they would hold cattle.

One day, I rode up on a dirt tank and saw something that was real pink-colored on the ground and went over to check it out. I stepped off my horse and looked down. It was a half-set of somebody's false teeth. I put them in my pocket and then hollered at Juan, who was helping me, and told him to come over there. I showed him the teeth and told him there might be a dead man somewhere close by, and we went to looking for a body.

We never found one; so we went back, loaded our horses, and headed home. On the way out, I saw Sherman Bell driving down the gravel road, so I stopped him and told him about the teeth.

He said, "Oh hell, Old Man Strapper and I were running a bunch of cattle up there a few years back. He put his teeth in his shirt pocket 'cause they'd sometimes fall out when he went to hollering and running his horse. We caught those cows, but he'd lost his teeth in the chase. We looked for 'em for a week and never found 'em."

I said, "Well, here they are," and gave them to him.

He mailed them to the old feller, and I got a real nice thank-you note from him a couple of weeks later. He said he sure appreciated it, but that five years in the hot sun had drawn them up and they didn't fit too good anymore.

After we got all the fences checked, I got a crew to help me move cattle from a place I had leased outside Ft. Stockton over to Pinto Canyon. I had about 200 mother cows, and a lot of them had calves; so I hired a couple of big 18-wheel cattle trucks to help us haul.

That first morning when we got down there, those drivers took one look at that gravel road dropping off into Pinto Canyon and said they would have to unload up on top because they couldn't get to the bottom. We didn't have any horses with us, and we had to turn all those cattle out on the road, and they just took off on trails down into the canyon.

Chris Spenser who was helping me was pretty young and athletic. He and I started walking down behind the cattle trying to get them to the bottom and on water. All of a sudden, I saw Chris just stop in his tracks and freeze.

We hadn't known anything about it, but there were eight Marines stationed up on top of that hill watching for drug smugglers. They were under a camouflage net, and Chris had walked right into the middle of them. He said when he stopped, he had eight rifles pointed right at him.

They wanted to know what he was doing there, and he told them; so they called their commander on the radio to make sure it was okay for us to be there. These were kids right out of the city who had probably never seen a cow, much less country like Pinto Canyon.

Chris scared them, and they scared him, and we were lucky no one got shot that day.

We got the other cattle there the next day and finally got everything settled down and scattered out.

I knew when I leased the ranch that the owners had it for sale. I had a two month get-off clause; so I figured if I had to, I could get my cattle off the place.

One day Chip Cole, a real estate broker, called me and said he had a potential buyer he was bringing down. He said he didn't know the ranch that well and asked me if I would meet him and help him show this feller around. I told him I would, and the next day he came down with a feller named Jeff Fort and his daughter Elizabeth. We drove all over the ranch, and I told him everything I knew about the place.

At one point, Jeff asked me if I would be interested in continuing to lease the ranch if he bought it. I told him I would and was glad when he ended up buying it. He is a number-one feller, and we've been friends ever since.

Roping a Saddle

When I first leased Pinto Canyon, Bee Pearce and Sam Dove had some cattle on a place that bordered me. They had lost their lease and had gathered all but about 10 head of their cattle.

Bee asked me what I'd charge to go in and catch those cattle, and I told him I'd do it on halves of whatever I caught. He said okay, so I got a couple of boys that worked for me, and we went after them.

We found the cattle in the bottom of a draw that Sam had told me he didn't think there was any way out of. I'd lived all my life in this country, and I'd seen very few true box canyons that you couldn't get out of. I figured those cows knew a way out. So we fell in behind them and trailed them down the canyon.

There was a little bitty trail that they went down, and we came up on a place where there was a big oak limb about four feet off the ground with no way around it.

We could see where the cows had been crawling under it from the hair they left on the limb. We unsaddled our horses, and two of us got under the limb and pushed as hard as we could to lift it. The other two fellers took the horses under, one leading and one popping them on the rump with the bridle reins to get them under.

We saddled back up, and finally found the cattle in a cat claw thicket right on the fence line of a county road that ran through Pinto Canyon. The first one to break and run was a big rogue steer that was kind of the ring leader, so I ran up and roped him. We got seven head roped and tied down, but lost three. We were able to get the fence down and get a truck and trailer on the road to load them up.

About a week later, I went back with my son David and his friend Sid Stevens. I let Sid ride a good little paint horse I had and use one of my saddles. This time I had a pack of dogs with me to get those cattle out of the cat claw.

We rode in and sure enough, those cattle went right back to that same spot. There was a Braford bull in the bunch that would weigh about 1,300 or 1,400 pounds. He broke and ran first.

Well, Sid bailed in behind him on that paint horse, but he'd forgotten to tighten his cinch before he went to rope. He dropped a loop right over that bull's horns and waved his slack, and his horse sat right down to stop that bull. Sid, saddle, bridle, and everything went right over that horse's head, just like you'd squirt a seed out of a prune.

I saw what happened and saw my good saddle bouncing along behind that bull on the end of a rope, so I went after the bull. I'd get up almost close enough to throw, and that saddle would bounce about 10 feet in the air, and my horse would duck off, trying to get away from the saddle. So I finally just backed off and roped the saddle.

When I got my horse stopped, I had that bull on 30 feet of my rope and 30 feet of Sid's rope—out there on 60 feet of rope, jumping like a sailfish.

David ran up and got another rope on the bull. When he went tight with his rope, his cinch broke right in two. He and his saddle went flying off his horse.

So now I've got the bull, three ropes, and two saddles all flopping around on the ground and in the air. I told David that I'd try to keep the bull off him if he'd get his saddle loose from his rope, and then try to get the other saddle loose and make one good rig out of the two.

The other boys were down chasing the other cattle and had no idea what we were going through.

Finally, David got a saddle put together and a horse caught and saddled. We got the bull tied down after a pretty good fight and then went over to where the other fellers were. They had caught all the other cattle, so we went to get the truck and trailer to load them.

When we went to load the bad bull we had tied down, he was a good way from the trailer. David and I both got ropes on him, and I had Juan ready to untie the pigging string holding the bull's legs together.

I told David that we were going to have to go through a draw to get to the road, and it was about 10 feet deep. I told him when we hit the top of that draw to really give it all he had down the side, so we could pull that bull up the other side because I knew that bull would be fighting the ropes.

We got there and both spurred our horses down the side and were headed back up when David's old saddle broke right in two. He went flying off the back of the horse. Just as he went off, that horse planted both hind feet right in his chest.

I could tell he was hurt, so I went hard left with the bull trying to keep it off of David. One of the Mexican men helping us ran to help David and drag him out of the way.

We finally got the bull and the other cattle loaded. David wasn't hurt too bad, but he had two big horseshoe prints on his chest for a while.

Tired Bull

Jeff Fort, who bought Pinto Canyon Ranch, had never been with us roping wild cattle, so he went along one morning to get one of the last bulls off the ranch. We spotted this big gray bull up on the side of a mountain eating prickly pear. I told Frankie Galvan and Jeff to wait down on the road, and I would go up and see if I could work him off the mountain down to the road.

When I got up to him, he didn't want to go anywhere. Every time I'd get close, he'd start pawing the ground and then run at me. I hollered for Frankie to come up to where I was on the side of the mountain, and we started agitating him. One of us would get him to charge us, and then the other one would run up to him and he'd charge him.

Finally, I guess he'd had enough. He bailed off the side of that mountain running full speed. We were right behind him. As soon as he hit the road at the bottom, Frankie got a rope on him, and I got a second rope on him. He just went flat down on the ground.

It took us an hour and a half to load him because he just laid there and never made an effort to get up or fight. I had an 8,000-pound winch in the front of my trailer, so we put a chain around his horns and just winched him into the trailer. He never did get up.

He was taking up so much room, we just pulled his head up tight against the front of the trailer and loaded a horse on top of him for the trip to town. When we got home with him, we unloaded the horse off of him and untied that bull, but he just laid there. I hit him with a hot shot, and he dang near tore the trailer apart.

He wasn't hurt a bit. He was just resting.

Down South with Ben Benavides

There is a road that heads south out of Marfa and ends up on the Rio Grande at a little spot in the road called Ruidosa. About 30 miles out of Marfa, it changes from being paved to gravel and then drops off into Pinto Canyon.

That road has been a smugglers' route for a couple of hundred years and goes through some of the roughest country in West Texas. The road goes right through the middle of Pinto Canyon Ranch and, south of that, through Ben Benavides' ranch.

I had a deal with Ben to gather wild cattle off his place on halves. We went over there one day and spotted a little bunch of cows on top of a mountain. We rode up and pushed them off to lower ground, so we could get trucks to them when we got them roped. There was a great big bull in the bunch. I guess he figured out what was happening and turned and ran back up the side of the mountain.

I was riding a big, stout horse named Mr. Ed, and I got the bull roped before he could get away. I hollered at the other boys helping me to get those cattle down to the bottom and get them tied down.

About the time Pat Yeager was riding over to help me with the big bull, it made a run at me, and Mr. Ed didn't move quite fast enough. The bull hooked him and took some hide off but didn't really hurt the horse. Pat got another rope on him, and we got him tied down.

We rode up to where we could see the other boys, and they had all but one of their cattle tied down. The loose one was about a 1,200-pound bull that had run up the side of another mountain onto a really steep little ledge. We were able to ride up and get just above him, so we could try to force him to go down.

Justin Clinton had a .22 pistol with rat shot, and I told him to shoot the bull in the butt and get him moving one way or the other. Justin shot him, and that bull came straight up the mountain toward us. When he came by me, I roped him and started down the hill.

Before he even took the slack out of my rope, he whirled around and came back down on my other side. I never had time to try and get the rope to the other side of me, and it was tied hard to the saddle horn. I knew I had to stay in front of that damn bull until I could get the rope over my head and to the other side, or I was going to be in big trouble.

About that time, Mr. Ed came up on a 3- or 4-foot-deep draw on the side of the mountain and slammed on the brakes. The bull never even slowed down, and he put a world-class trip on us. Mr. Ed turned a flip, and I landed head-first in a big bunch of boulders.

I jumped up trying to see where the bull was and started running, but I ran straight into the rope. It was about boot-top high, and I slammed into the rocks a second time.

The bull started working on Mr. Ed while he was still down and messed him up pretty bad. The other boys finally got a couple of ropes on the bull, and we got him down to the road and loaded in the trailer.

I told the boys that I was hurt, and my horse was sure hurt, and for one of them to take us to town. We took the horse to the vet, and they had to put 70 or 80 stitches in him. Then they took me to the hospital, and they put a bunch of stitches in my head where it was busted open from the rocks.

I think the hospital and vet bills were more than I made on my half of the cattle, which is about par for the course.

Wreck in the Kitchen

Roddy Schoenfield had been ranching on Elephant Mountain for quite some time, and things got real dry. He finally decided he would move all his cattle to a ranch up by Mason in Central Texas, and I went down to help him gather and ship.

Loading cattle on those big 18-wheelers is like making sausage; it's probably better if you don't watch. We had more cows than the trucks were really supposed to hold, so we had to put some of the smaller cows up in what they call the "kitchen." It has a lower ceiling and is usually used to haul small calves.

One old high-horn cow ended up in there while we were loading, and we just left her. When we got to Mason, we were unloading in the dark and using flashlights. That one cow got hung up and couldn't get out of the kitchen.

Sam Dove and I went in and were doing our best to get her out. She went to fighting us, and she hooked me right under the eye and tore my cheek and the side of my head open pretty good.

The truck driver opened a little trap door to the kitchen from the outside of the truck, took one look at me, and said, "Oh my God, she's done hooked his eyeball out!"

I knew I had a bunch of blood all over me, so I closed one eye and then the other. I could still see, so I figured if my eyeball was out, it must still be working.

The cow finally scrambled out of the trailer, and Roddy took me into Mason to the hospital.

They put 8 stitches in my face, and my eyeball was still in the socket. I was sore for a few days, and my head was swollen up pretty good size, but I was sure glad to still have both headlights working.

Stripping the Inspector Down

Johnny Fitzgerald from over at Ft. Davis called one day and said that the lady he was running a ranch for wanted someone to get all the goats off the place. She said she would sell them for $10 a head in the pasture, so I told him I'd come get them.

I took a couple of good hands with me, and a feller that was the local government livestock inspector wanted to go with us, too. He was a big, heavy-set feller and didn't do much work ahorseback. But I loaned him one of my old roping horses, and we took him along anyway.

Those goats got way up in some rough rock slides that we couldn't get our horses in. We left the inspector on his horse, tied our horses, and went afoot up to get those goats off the mountain. When the goats came down, they came 90-to-nothing, and we were all scrambling to get to our horses, so we could try to pen them.

When those goats ran right by my old roping horse, he knew he was supposed to follow what was running; so he took off like a scalded dog.

They went through a brush thicket with some trees in it, and that inspector disappeared into it, holding on for dear life. When he came out the other side, he didn't have anything left but his britches and his boots. His hat and shirt were completely gone, and he was scratched and bleeding all over. Just as he was almost out, he hit a big limb that caught his belly and flipped him off the horse backward. He was a mess, but he didn't have anything broken.

We got the goats gathered and took them to Alpine. I averaged $80 a head on them when I sold them, so I came out pretty good. And I guess that old boy had a story to tell his grandkids someday.

We were up in that same country around Ft. Davis not long after that, helping another friend work his cattle. Bangs disease was pretty bad then, so everyone had to test their cattle every couple of months.

Those cows got to where they didn't want to get in the chute because they knew they were going to get a bunch of needles stuck in them. We had one pretty good-sized bull that had knocked the gate down and was raising all kinds of hell about going into the chute. So the foreman hollered at me to rope that so-and-so.

The bull weighed 1,700 or 1,800 pounds, and my little gray horse Dusty probably didn't weigh 900 pounds. But I roped the bull. We were right next to a fence when the bull hit the end of the rope and jerked my horse backward into that fence.

I stepped off as quick as I could but ended up under the horse. Ol' Dusty held that bull, and I was able to get out from under him, but that wreck broke my saddle tree in the process.

Several other boys came and got ropes on the bull, and we got him worked without anyone getting hurt. But if I hadn't stepped off when I did, that fence would have sure made a mess out of me.

Legal Cattle Rustling

Back in the early '90s, Jerry Alcon was the local inspector for the USDA. Part of his job was to make sure any Mexican cattle that crossed into the U.S. were caught. His government agency neutered both cows and bulls, quarantined them for a specified period, and then sold them.

He called me one day and said that a couple of ranchers in the Langtry area were complaining about a lot of Mexican cattle crossing over onto their ranches. They were having a hard time gathering them, and he wanted to know if I would go give it a shot.

I got a couple of my boys together, and we went down there early one morning. We unloaded right by the Rio Grande and immediately saw fresh tracks coming out of the river. One of the boys hollered, and we saw a bunch of cattle going up the hill on the U.S. side and ran our horses to them.

The bull in the bunch kept going up the hill, but the cows and calves broke back down toward the river. I yelled that I would get the bull and for the rest of the men to go after the others.

I was riding a big sorrel horse named Playboy that I had just traded for. I could tell by the way he stopped that he hadn't had many big cattle roped on him because he didn't stop on his rear end and drop it. I figured he'd have to learn that trick pretty quick if he was going to make it with our crew.

I roped that bull, and the horse stopped him; but the bull kept moving the horse who wouldn't drop that rear end and park. The bull kept dragging us toward an old fence, and finally he ran over it.

He kept lunging, and my horse kept giving until the horse's legs got tangled in the downed fence.

I should have stepped off, but I didn't, and the horse went down with me under him. When I was able to get out from under the horse, I looked down and saw an interesting sight. My left little finger was touching my left elbow. I grabbed ahold of my wrist and jerked it back straight and then stuck it into the front of my shirt.

Doing that will get your full attention!

The bull came back over the fence and jerked the rope, which pulled the horse back on his feet, but the saddle was pulled over to the side pretty far. The bull and the horse were tied together.

I was off about 40 yards watching the show.

The bull ran at the horse, and somehow when ol' Playboy dodged the bull, the bull stepped over the rope. When the horse hit the end of the rope again, he threw a trip[33] and busted the bull.

I ran over to the horse and with my right arm loosened the cinch enough to get the saddle back up straight. Then I threw the latigo over my shoulder and tightened it as tight as I could. I reached down and tightened the flank cinch.

But about that time, the bull got his wind back. He got up, and I got out of the way. I got up on a hill and took my little binoculars out of my leggings pocket and looked down to see if the other boys had caught all the cattle.

Justin Clinton had a cow roped and just got her tied down when the dogs ran her calf right into him. He just grabbed the calf and bulldogged it and tied it down, too. These boys didn't have any back-up in them; they were sure enough good hands.

When things settled down, I hollered for them to come up to where I was. They saw my horse and the bull tied together and got another rope on the bull and tied him down. When we finally got all the cattle loaded in the trailer, we headed for Alpine.

I had broken that arm just before 8 A.M. It was almost 6 P.M. before the doctor got it taken care of. He said when I pulled it, I had set it

---

33   Trip - When an animal is roped by the horns or head and the rope pulls tight and trips a foot, throwing the animal to the ground.

just about as good as it could have been set by a doctor. Sure was lucky there, but that sure hadn't keep it from hurting pretty bad. I had chewed a couple of mesquite roots up before we got to town.

At the time, I was in the lead to win the buckle in the Coors team-roping series in Ft. Stockton. If you're over 55 years old, they'll let you tie on to the saddle horn in the team-roping instead of dallying like most people do.

I was worried because they were going to have the next roping about two weeks after I broke my arm. I had a pretty good lead on the number two header, but to qualify I had to participate in every roping in the series. So I cut my rope down short and was able to hold a couple of coils of rope and my bridle reins with the part of my fingers hanging out of the cast.

I had a real good horse I called Dunny, and he put me right where I needed to be every time. We not only won the roping that day but cinched the buckle for the series.

Ol' Dunny and I had won lots of buckles and a few saddles together, and he had won top horse in several events over the years. He was probably the best all-around ranch and roping horse I ever owned.

This all happened in April. In February of the next year, Jerry Alcon called me and wanted me to go back down there and look for more cattle. I took Frankie Galvan and some other fellers, and we ended up roping and tying down 28 head off those ranches.

These weren't the average, scrawny Mexican cattle. One steer weighed almost 1,800 pounds, and Frankie roped a big Braford bull that weighed 1,400 pounds.

When we roped the biggest steer in the bunch, a feller who worked for me named Juan and I jumped him in a little bunch of cattle.

Juan ran after the steer but missed his first loop. I was right behind him and caught the steer, but I had him by the horns. You always try to rope cattle like that around the neck, so you can choke them down.

Apache riding Dunny at a roping

Juan came in and heeled him, but when we stretched him out, Juan's old rope broke.

So I just had him by the horns again. He kept running at me; but I was riding a good little horse, and we stayed one step ahead of him and kept trying to trip him. I guess we'd been roping too many cattle, and our ropes were wearing out in that brush because my rope broke, too.

We had some dogs with us, and they circled that steer and kept him busy while I got another rope. Juan tied another honda[34] in his rope, and we finally got both ends of that bull roped. That was one of the stoutest and most athletic animals I ever roped.

---

34   honda - The small tied loop in a rope that the tail of the rope is run through to form a sliding loop.

Stinkin' Goats and Broken Bones

One day a friend of mine told me about a feller named Steve Baker who had bought a ranch down around Langtry. He said Steve had a whole bunch of wild goats that he wanted to get off the place. He gave me Steve's name and phone number, and I called him.

He said, yeah, he sure wanted to get rid of those goats. He had hired several people to try and catch them; but they hadn't had much luck. I told him I thought I could get them gathered, and I met him down there the next day to look things over.

He had about 20 sections of the roughest old slick-rock country around, and we saw 400-500 head of goats on it. His ranch had several miles of the Rio Grande running through it, and you needed a sure-footed horse to work it. A shod horse would hit one of those big slick-rock areas and be like a cow on roller skates.

I made a deal with him and went back and got a crew of men together that I knew could work that kind of country.

We set up panels to try and pen the goats in and went to work. The first morning, we had about 100 head gathered and brought the goats to the pens. They went in the pens all right, but then went right over the top of those panels, just like deer. I'd never seen a bunch of goats that could jump like that.

We were pretty disgusted and were headed back to the house to come up with another plan when we rode up on another bunch of goats. There were four of us, and we all had several pigging strings each, so we just went to roping. We got 19 roped and tied down in just a few minutes. I told those boys we were going to Plan B—we'd just rope them and forget trying to pen any.

We went back two more times and roped 70-80 goats each time. We'd put them in trailers and take them to the shipping pens, which were tall enough to hold them in.

Then, Steve told us that there were a bunch of Mexican cattle that had crossed over onto his place. The USDA was paying to catch those cattle, so we found them and roped them, too. We made a pretty good payday out of that.

When we went back the next time, our luck changed. We were running a bunch of goats down the side of a draw that was full of slick rock at the bottom.

A college boy from Nebraska that worked for me named Ryan Ruther (we called him The Nebraska Flash) was just about to rope a goat when his horse hit that slick rock. That horse's legs went in four different directions, and Flash hit the rock and shattered his elbow.

I was up on top chasing a big Billy goat, and my horse fell. When I hit the ground, I ran a greasewood stob halfway through my forearm. I jerked it out, got back on my horse, and got the goat roped that I was chasing. Those Billys were bigger than the nannys and would bring more money, so we tried to get them first. I tied him, threw him over the front of my saddle, and carried him back to the trailer.

John Duerkop was with us, and he took Flash to Del Rio to get his arm fixed. We worked another couple of days chasing goats. We got a bunch more caught and took them up to Junction to the sale barn and went home.

After a few days, my arm really started bothering me where that stob had gone in. It didn't smell all that good either. I was coming home from the ranch one day, and called Joy on my cell phone. I told her she better make me an appointment with the doctor because the smell was so bad I was having to drive with my arm out the window to keep from throwing up.

I went to her office, and she took me straight to the emergency room. They took one look and put me in the hospital. I was in there for 6 days with them trying to get the infection under control.

I think having that open wound and handling all those stinking old goats probably gave me something the doctors had never seen before.

Where Am I?

Sam Caviness was working for a feller named Bill Sole, and things got pretty dry. They needed to ship some cattle they had on a leased place down south of Elephant Mountain. He called and wanted me to help them, so I went down there.

They had some small pens that wouldn't hold all the cattle, so we had to hold a bunch of the cattle up in a corner of one of the pastures. We were riding through them a lot trying to straighten them out, and by the end of the day they were getting pretty ringy.[35]

I was riding a young dun horse I was training when a big calf broke out and ran off.

Sam and I took off and roped and tied him down and were riding back to the herd when a big cow broke out. She ran right between us going about 90 miles an hour, and I just dropped my loop on her when she went by.

Before I could get the little horse turned around, she hit the end of the rope and jerked that dun horse right over backwards

I landed under him, hitting head first. It knocked me colder than a wedge.

They got the cow tied down and caught my horse, and about that time another feller drove up in his pickup. They got him to drive me to town. He took me home and put me on my couch, but I was still knocked out.

Bill Sole had called his wife after we left the ranch and told her to go by the house and check on me. She found me unconscious and somehow got me in the car and to the hospital.

Joy was helping put on a roping over in Ft. Stockton; and they finally found her, and she came to the hospital. She ran into a nurse she knew who told her what room I was in, and she asked the nurse why it took so long for them to call her. Joy said, "Apache knew where I was."

That nurse said, "Hell, Apache doesn't know where he is, much less where you were."

---

35   ringy - Wild and upset.

She got to the room and saw they had me all hooked up with wires and tubes. I had just come to and was asking Dr. Pearce what had happened. When he said, "You fell off your horse," I told him, "Doc, a lot of things might have happened, but I guarantee you I didn't just fall off my horse."

They kept me a couple of days, but there wasn't anything wrong but a little bit of scrambled brains.

The Wild and Wooly 02 Ranch

The 02 Ranch was about 25 miles south of Alpine, and covered 450 sections. The Nunnley brothers had it leased for years, but in the mid-nineties they lost their lease. They went in with a crew of cowboys and gathered all the cattle they could. Then they got helicopters to gather the rest.

They got down to where they thought there were only about 30 or 40 head left, and it wasn't worth paying the helicopters to stay and chase them.

Bill Kennedy, who was running the ranch for them, called and asked me if I'd be interested in going halves and trying to gather the rest of the cattle. I said I would and put together a crew of some young fellers that I'd known most of their lives and had kinda trained them. I had Frankie Galvan, Pat Yeager, Justin Clinton, Flash (Ryan Ruther), and my boy David.

We ended up gathering 178 cows and bulls. Some of those bulls weighed over 2,000 pounds and had probably never seen a man. Some of those little horses we were riding weighed about 900 pounds, so when you had a big bull roped, you'd better be paying attention.

We penned two and roped and tied down all the rest. Not many were headed-and-heeled either. They were roped and tied down by one man because the other men were busy trying to get cows tied down that they had roped.

The first three days, those boys broke a cow's leg every day because they were running in there and roping them and then throwing a trip on them. When you trip a cow, you rope the head, throw the slack in your rope to the right of the cow, and then turn your horse to the left as hard as you can go. The rope pulls the cow's head down between its feet and flips it over hard.

That was costing me a lot of money, so that next morning I told them we had a new deal. I would give them a third of my half of the money on all the cows we caught, which would be a lot more for each of them. Not another cow got a broken leg after that.

One day, Frankie and Pat had a pretty snorty cow roped and were trying to drag her into the trailer. They had their ropes run through the trailer and were on their horses trying to pull the cow up into the trailer. She was lying flat down with her feet behind her, and they couldn't get her up into the back of the trailer.

I'd always preached to those boys to never get into the"V" between two ropes because it was a real dangerous place. But this old cow was so strung out, I figured I could get in there and lift her head up to get her started into the trailer without a problem.

Well, she was on her feet and hooking at me in a heartbeat, and I ran to get out of the way. When I jumped to get over one of the ropes, my toe caught, and I went down like a tripped steer. It just about knocked me out, and those boys tied that cow where she was and came to check on me.

I hit face down on the rocks and pealed a strip of hide from between my eyes to the end of my nose. It was just hanging down like a banana peel. I told Frankie to grab that piece of hide and jerk it off, but he said he wasn't about to.

When I looked around, all the other boys had left me and were back getting on their horses. They weren't interested in getting that hide off either. So I went over to the mirror on the pickup, pulled out my pocket knife, and cut that strip of hide off my nose.

I've never seen such a tough bunch of cowboys back off from something that fast. But those boys were really top hands, and I'd go after just about anything on four feet with them. Later on for the USDA, we gathered a lot of wild cattle and cattle crossing the river.

Some time after we'd finished gathering the wild cattle at the 02 Ranch, Bill Kennedy called me again and said they had seen the tracks of a big bull that we must have missed. So one day, I got Frankie Galvan, and we loaded a couple of horses and some dogs and went down there.

I'd bought a horse that came out of Mexico, but he was a pretty good kind of a horse. He had a big sunken-in place in the side of his head, so we called him Dent. He was a good ranch horse and just as gentle as a dog.

Right before we were going to the 02 again, a feller I knew called me and told me he had a real nice sorrel 6-year-old registered horse that just kept pitching with him. He was an older feller, and he said he'd trade me that horse for a gentle one, so I traded him Dent.

Frankie took the new sorrel horse when we went back to the 02 looking for that bull. We rode for several hours looking for the bull or for his tracks. We finally found some tracks that looked like they weren't too old and unloaded our horses. After we spread out looking for that bull, I found some real fresh tracks and called Frankie on the little two-way radios we'd started carrying.

When Frankie was about 150 yards from me, one of the dogs jumped a big banana-horned bull out of a thicket. He weighed 1,800 to 2,000 pounds, and he left there like a thoroughbred horse out the starting gate. I ran and tried to rope him, but my loop bounced off his horns.

Frankie was on him and roped him just as he went down into a little draw. His horse jumped the draw and was trying his best to hold that bull. He never offered to pitch. I guess he had his wagon loaded, and he knew it.

I came over and got another rope on him, and we got him tied down. It took us forever to get the truck and trailer into where we had him roped, but we finally got it there and got him loaded.

You know, a lot of people call themselves cowboys, but when you can take a horse that somebody else can't ride and go out and rope a full-grown wild bull and get him tied down, now that's a cowboy in my book. There aren't many that can stay with Frankie Galvan ahorseback.

New Ranch, More Broken Bones

In 2004, Joy and I bought a ranch south of Ft. Stockton. Although we live in town, I'm at the ranch most days. Pete, the Mexican feller who's been with me for years, lives there full-time. I thought that would help me kinda settle down and stay out of trouble, but I guess it didn't.

In early 2008, the Cowboy Church in Ft. Stockton was having a roping one Sunday afternoon and asked me to come flag for them. I took a young horse I was training and figured it would be good for the horse to be around a little excitement. When I got there, they needed another header for the roping, so instead of flagging, I entered up. The horse hadn't been to a roping before but did okay for the first couple of steers. Then we came out of the header's box.

When I stood up to rope, the horse just disappeared out from under me. I hit the ground, broke my pelvic girdle in seven places, and ended up in the hospital in Lubbock.

After a couple of days in the hospital and a lot of head scratching, the doctors told me that the best thing I could do was to go home and stay in bed for two months to let it heal. I did that and slowly got back on my feet. But my hip wasn't right. I had a bad limp, could barely get in and out of my truck, and sure couldn't ride a horse.

That went on for a year and a half, with things getting only a little better. Finally I went to my doctor and said, "I don't care if you cut this right leg off, but I gotta have some relief from the pain. And I want to get back on my horse."

He helped me find another doctor in Lubbock who said he could repair the hip socket that was basically still destroyed. This doctor had done a lot of work on soldiers hurt in Iraq and sure seemed to know what he was doing. The operation worked, and after some rehab and driving a few nurses crazy, I'm back on my horses and roping cattle again.

It's not real pretty watching me get on a horse these days; but once I'm on, I'm still pushing on those reins every chance I get.

Apache and Joy Adams, 2009

PART TWO
HE'LL DO TO RIDE THE RIVER WITH

The Author's Experiences
Riding with Apache Adams

Butch & Sundance

Coming down the side of a steep mountain in Pinto Canyon, Apache was just ahead of me. There wasn't a trail, and we'd gotten into a place where we were "bluffed out" and couldn't see anything below the bluff we stopped on.

Apache's horse's head was sticking out far enough that he could see over, and he wasn't interested in going any further.

I said, "Let's work our way around to the right a little more, and maybe there's a way down over there."

Yelling down to Flash Ruther, who had stayed down below us on the road, Apache said, "Flash, is there any place to land if I jump off this bluff?"

Flash looked for a long minute and then replied, "Well, if your horse can land on a little outcropping about six feet below the bluff, I think he can jump to the right and hit a pretty good slide and come on down."

Without another word, Apache spurred his horse and disappeared over the bluff.

Thunk...scramble, scramble, scramble.

Silence.

Thunk...scramble, slide...slide...more slide.

"Don," came the voice from below, "just be sure to jump right after you hit the first time, and lean waaaay back in the saddle."

Immediately, a vision of Butch and Sundance holding tightly to that gunbelt, jumping into the abyss, and yelling "Shi-i-i-it!" came to mind. I leaned back as far as I could and pushed my horse over the edge.

The Real Deal

I first met Apache Adams in 1990 when I came to Alpine for the Texas Cowboy Poetry Gathering. I had read about the event in a magazine and came to see what it was all about. I ended up getting invited to perform at the event the next year.

Apache was also one of the performers, captivating audiences with his great stories. There was no question in my mind that he was the real thing, and we soon struck up a friendship. Over the next few years, we got to know each other better at the Alpine Gathering and similar events in Lubbock and Ruidoso, New Mexico.

I had day-worked during spring roundups for the Kenneys on The D Ranch up near Guadalupe Pass, and Apache knew Mr. James Kenney pretty well. When I asked Apache if I could come help him work some cattle, he told me to come ahead.

Let me say loud and clear right here that I was no kind of working cowboy and never claimed to be. My grandfather was a good cowboy, my folks had owned a small ranch in Central Texas, and I owned a few cattle myself. But that was a far cry from the life Apache had lived in the expanses of the Big Bend.

Apache always says that when he breaks a horse, he takes it from kindergarten straight to college and just leaves out elementary and high school. He does the same with people, and I soon found myself in places and doing things that most people only see in the movies.

At that time, he still had the country leased down near Terlingua that he called Adobe Walls. This is big, wide-open country with lots of hills and mesas. Almost something you'd see in an old John Ford movie, but without the grass.

One day, we were moving some cattle that had gotten out into another ranch back into his pasture. It was just the two of us, and when we got them through the gate, they broke into a fast trot. I stepped off my horse to close the gate, and Apache yelled for me to hurry and get around them on the other side, so we could get them back under control.

I jumped on my horse, and we took off running to get around the cattle. When I rode up on a big draw, I slowed my horse a little, went through the arroyo, and then ran around and slowed the cattle.

When we got them where we wanted them and were riding back to the truck and trailer, Apache said, "How come you slowed down when you went through that draw while ago?"

I told him it looked pretty rough and steep, and I didn't want to kill myself.

He said, "Oh hell, let the horse watch the ground. Don't ever look down, or it'll scare you to death."

That was just the beginning!

The author and Apache working cattle, 2010

Grub and Wood Stoves

Branding a bunch of cattle one day, Apache said, "Go over to my truck, and bring some more vaccine. It's in a paper sack behind the seat."

Pulling the pickup seat forward, I uncovered Fibber McGee's closet...cowboy style. Digging through old jackets, bug spray cans, a cattle prod, and various tool and windmill parts, I kept coming across food cans with the labels worn off. One had part of a label left, and it was full of hominy.

I finally found the medicine and took it over to where Apache had a bawling calf roped by the heels and was dragging him to the fire.

We finished the branding work, and I walked up to Apache while he was loosening the girth on his horse. "You sure must like hominy," I said.

"Oh hell, I hate the stuff," he replied.

I said, "Well, how come there's about 6 or 8 cans of it behind the seat of your truck?"

"Oh, that's my emergency rations. If I put something back there that I like, I'll eat it!"

Not long after that, Apache called one morning and said, "If you want to come out next weekend, we're going to try to catch some wild cattle running down by the river."

We were saddling up way before daylight, and I asked Apache, "Do you think we'll be coming back to camp for lunch, or will we be out all day?"

He said, "We'll probably be out all day unless we run into those cattle pretty quick and get 'em roped. I think we're going to have to track them to find them. But don't worry, I've got us a lunch packed."

About one in the afternoon, we stopped by a little trickle of water in a creek bed, and Apache said it was lunch time. He gave each man a tortilla and then opened a can of Ranch Style Beans with his pocket knife. We held out our tortillas, and he put a dab of beans on it. We got a drink from the creek and took off looking for more cattle.

People find it hard to believe that most cowboys don't carry water with them when they're horseback. A canteen would bounce and flop all around when they were running after a cow, so it's not unusual to go 6 or 8 hours without water if they don't find a creek or horse trough.

Riding along beside him ahorseback, I smiled and said, "Boy, Adams! You keep feeding me like that, and I'll get fat and lazy on you."

He looked over at me and grinned. "Hell, we came to work, not to get fat. The difference between plain food and a gourmet meal is a couple-a hours of hard work. You ever notice that?"

Years later, when Apache and I had the Pinto Canyon Ranch leased from Jeff Fort, we were preparing to spend several days at the ranch gathering and working cattle. We had hired some men to help us and were at the grocery store in Alpine buying food for the crew.

I was pushing the cart, and Apache was throwing things in. I said, "I guess I should have made a list since we'll be feeding 5 or 6 men for several days. I don't want anybody to go hungry."

Apache said, "I got a list in my head...tortillas, meat, and beans."

He threw 8 or 10 dozen flour tortillas into the cart, then he started throwing in plastic packages of bologna and salami, the ones with all the white fat showing through the plastic.

I was putting them back as fast as he could put them in the basket. I said, "We can go to the deli and get fresh-cut lunch meat that would be a lot better and probably not cost any more."

"Damn, you're sure picky," came his reply.

At the deli, I said to the guy behind the counter, "Give us a couple of pounds each of smoked turkey and ham."

In his best "pasture voice" Apache blurted out, "Hell no! We don't want no damn turkey. We're in the cattle bidness. Give us the ham!"

We got our groceries and went on to camp.

Pinto Canyon is some of the roughest country in West Texas. When I had a bunch of cattle that I'd bought hauled from Central Texas to Pinto Canyon, the guy driving the truck told me later, "Man, I was driving along those big grass flats outside Marfa thinking I'd gone to heaven. Then I dropped off into Pinto Canyon and thought I was headed into hell."

We had a little one-room tin building that we stayed in at Pinto Canyon. We called it the "microwave." It was burning hot in the summer and like a locker plant in the winter. And it got pretty exciting in the middle of the night when the ringtail cat[36] that lived there went running across the bedrolls.

One morning way before daylight, I was cooking breakfast and could hear Adams rattling around back by the wood stove. He mumbled, "Damn I hate the cold, but I'll fix that."

Then came the explosion. It blew the front and the back doors to the building wide open.

When I figured out that I was still in one piece, I looked back toward the stove. Apache's grandson, Dusty, was still little and kept several Teddy Bears back by his bed. The stove was bellowing smoke and a couple of Teddy Bears were on fire. I yelled, "Apache, are you okay?"

He said, "Oh I'm great. It took a gallon of gasoline, but I got this damn stove lit."

Lost Horses

I've hunted all my life, and understand something about animal tracks and tracking. But before I started riding with Apache, I never imagined tracking horses or cattle for miles across desert terrain.

Apache and I had spent the night in a little trailer he had down at Adobe Walls. We planned on getting an early start that morning gathering a bunch of his cows.

He said, "You start breakfast, and I'm going to take my new 4-wheeler and gather the horses."

I said, "That Japanese wrangle horse you traded for looks like a wreck waiting to happen. Try to keep the rubber part down."

36   ringtail cat - A small cat-like wild animal with a very long tail having black rings around the entire length.

He had a horse trap that was about 1,000 acres, and we had penned the horses in there for the night. I made coffee, cooked breakfast, and it got cold, and he still wasn't back. I figured he'd wrecked the Honda and was bleeding in some arroyo when I heard the whine of the engine coming my way.

He roared up to the porch, and I said, "What's up? Where are the horses?"

He said, "The fence is down on the back side of the horse trap, and all 8 horses are long gone."

"How big is the pasture they got into?"

He said, "Oh, about 2 million acres. They call it Big Bend National Park!"

We ate breakfast and started out to find our horses. He took the 4-wheeler, and I followed in the pickup. I stayed on the few dirt roads I could find in the pickup, and Apache went cross-country on the 4-wheeler, tracking the horses.

About two o'clock that afternoon, we spotted our horses way off in the distance. Apache said, "You stay right here in the truck. I'm going way around them and try to get them started back in the direction of the ranch."

He finally got around them on the Honda and was bouncing across the rocks and cactus herding them back to the ranch. He came by me 90-to-nothing with a herd of horses thundering ahead of him. He ran them that way for several miles and then just stopped in the middle of the road.

I pulled up beside him and said, " How come you stopped? Did the Honda break down?"

He said, "I put a lot of pressure on those horses, and they're looking for relief. They'll be waiting for us at the gate to our pasture."

Sure enough, when we got to the gate, the horses were milling in a tight bunch, waiting to go through. When I opened it, they gratefully ran into the pasture.

Bucked Off

When Apache was gathering wild goats off of Steve Baker's ranch down near Langtry, he called me and asked if I wanted to meet him there and rope some goats. I showed up late one Friday night, and the next morning we were roping our horses before daylight. He led a little blue roan horse to me and said he was a young horse that needed some miles on him, but he'd been roped off of and shouldn't give me any trouble.

There were 6 or 8 of us working, and later that morning we found a pretty big bunch of goats. Apache yelled, "We need to try to pen those goats before we just run in and start roping. Push them toward the pens."

He looked at me and said, "You and Dusty follow me. We've go to get over those hills and block the gap, so the goats can't turn and go into another pasture."

We took off riding over some pretty big hills in a lope or a run trying to beat the goats. We road up on top of a really steep hill, and going down the other side was nothing but loose gravely rock.

Apache and Dusty, who was only about 6 or 7 at the time, went flying down the hill; but my little young horse balked and wouldn't go. I kept turning him down and crowding him hard to go down the hill. Finally, he just lunged off that hill taking big jumps.

I hadn't re-tightened my cinch that morning; so about the second jump, my saddle slid down onto that horse's neck, and he started to buck. We were going straight down the side of the hill, and I knew I was coming off. I just didn't want to get catapulted out into space.

As I went over his head, I grabbed his ears and flipped over his head. I landed on my back. My momentum took me for another summersault. When my feet hit again, I jumped sideways out of the horse's path. The little horse stopped at the bottom of the hill and just stood there.

I had the wind knocked out of me but finally got my breath and walked down the hill.

Dusty rode back and caught the horse, I adjusted the saddle, and we took off after Apache. I felt like someone had shot me in the back.

We worked the rest of the day, but my back was really giving me a fit. I slept in the bed of my truck on a foam pad that night. The next morning, I dang near couldn't get out of the truck. I didn't know it yet, but I had two cracked ribs. I went to the pen with them when they roped out their mounts about daylight.

Apache said, " Dusty, what horse are you going to ride today."

Dusty pointed at the little blue horse and said, "That one, Grandpa."

Apache said, "That's the one that bucked Don off yesterday."

Dusty had that crooked little smile on his face and replied, "I know."

When everyone was saddled and ready to go, Dusty stood up on top of his saddle holding the reins like a trick roper. He yelled over to me, "Looky here, Don."

Luckily for Dusty, I didn't have a pistol with me!

Almost Bucked Off

In the late '90s, Apache had a deal with the U.S. government to catch cattle and horses that were crossing the Rio Grande into Texas. There was danger of diseases coming into the country, and the Feds wanted it stopped.

One December, Apache called me and said, "Why don't you take a week off work and go down to the river south of Van Horn and catch Mexican cattle with me?"

How could I turn that offer down?

So Apache, Frankie Galvan, Pete, another fellow, and I took off for the river. We took horses, trailers, bedrolls, and a little bit of food and headed for some of the most remote ranches on the Rio Grande.

The author and Apache in the middle of the
Rio Grande near The River Ranch, late 1990s

One morning, we got up way before daylight, ate some of Pete's good tortillas, beans, and eggs, and saddled up. Apache said, "Saddle up that big stout bay horse over there, and come with me."

We were easing along in the dark, trying to get to some high ground before daybreak, so we could see the cattle grazing below us along the river. If we found some, we would ride down and rope them before they could cross back into Mexico. We came up to a little hill, and Apache said, "Let's lope up on that hill and wait for first light."

I put my horse into a lope, and he broke in two. I've never had a horse pitch that hard or that long, but somehow I stayed on him. When he finally stopped pitching, Apache said, "I believe that was the ugliest bronc ride I ever saw, but I'll give you a 10 since you don't have to walk back to camp."

I'd lost my hat in the mayhem and sure didn't want to have to climb off that horse and back on him to get it. I looked at Apache and said, "Do you mind getting my hat for me?"

He said with a grin, "I ain't getting your hat. You get it, and I might get to see another bronc ride before daylight."

I got the hat without incident, and the horse and I got along fine the rest of the day. But I sure was sucked up every time I had to spur him and run after a cow.

Swimming the Rio Grande

Jeff Fort and I were always fascinated with the stories Apache told about riding over the mountains and down into Marufo Vega when he was just a kid. He'd tell us how he would gather the cows and then have to push them all the way back down the Rio Grande, swimming the river a dozen times, to get them to the ranch.

We finally talked him into retracing his trip and taking us along. Apache said, "Use the lightest saddle blanket you've got, and don't wear boots. They'll fill up with water and drown you."

So we hauled three horses down to the old River Ranch. We each packed a sandwich and a bottle of water. Before we saddled up and left out right at 7 A.M. on a beautiful, sunny West Texas morning.

I was riding a little horse Apache called Spark Plug. He had a normal-sized body, but his legs were way too short for his body. He liked to crow-hop around when he was first saddled, but he couldn't buck a fat woman off if he tried. And he was as sure-footed as any mule.

We rode up and over some steep mountain trails and rough country. Apache hadn't ridden this trail in 50 years, but he found and followed it like he'd ridden it last week.

At one point, as we were going up a steep and narrow trail, he said, "Mother and Dad used to ride over this trail pulling a pack horse behind them. They would go all the way down to the Hot Springs in Big Bend Park where there was a little store. They'd stock up on provisions and ride back to the ranch."

Apache showing Jeff Fort and the author the trail to Marufo Vega
that he traveled regularly as a kid

About noon, we finally reached the river. We stopped, tied our horses for about 20 minutes, and ate our lunch.

Apache was looking down the river channel and said, "It looks like the cane has taken over the river banks since there aren't any cattle down here any more. We'd better get going. I think this is going to be tougher than we thought."

He was sure right. We would ride as far as we could on one side, and then when the cane was so thick we couldn't get through it, we'd swim the horses in the river until we could find a place to climb back up the bank.

At one point Apache warned us, "If your horse turns back toward you in that river, splash water in his face for all you're worth. He'll try to climb up on you like a dog would in the water and drown you with his front hooves."

We'd swim behind the horses, trying to hold onto their tails. But they usually outswam us and would find a place to climb up and be grazing on the bank when we got there.

At one point, old Spark Plug was swimming behind Apache's horse and somehow got part of the other horse's tail jammed between his horseshoe and his hoof. When they got out of the water, Spark Plug was hopping along behind the other horse on three legs with one foot in the horse's tail. That could have been a real wreck, but the horses stayed calm until we could get on the bank and get them untangled.

In some places, I was cutting the cane with the saw on my Leatherman tool so that we could push through. We'd get to a bank that was 8 or 10 feet above the water and slap the horses on the butt until they jumped off into the river. We'd jump off behind them, and the adventure would continue.

We finally got to The River Ranch and rode back to where we'd parked the trailer. I looked at my watch, and it was 7:05 P.M. We'd been gone for 12 hours, either riding or swimming all but 20 minutes of that.

Apache said, "Boys, that was a hell of a trip. I had no idea that cane had grown up like that. We're lucky one of us didn't drown on that little trip."

Loud Horse Whispering

Sometime around 2004, Apache and Joy bought a nice ranch south of Ft. Stockton. I helped them build a good set of working pens and did some remodeling work on the ranch houses.

One day while I was doing some carpenter work, Apache and Dusty led this horse up in front of the house. Dusty was 13 or 14 and already a heck of a cowboy, but not riding saddle broncs in rodeos yet.

Apache said, "I traded for this horse, and somebody really spoiled him. He rears up and just generally tries to fight you when you try to get on. I'm going to coach Dusty and see if he can work the problem out of the horse."

Dusty tried to mount a couple of times, and things were getting a little rough.

Apache finally said, "I think this horse might be more spoiled than I thought. Dusty, I don't want to get you hurt. Let me see what I can do with him."

Standing up by the horse's shoulder, Apache jerked the horse's head around. When the horse tried to rear up, Apache kicked him in the belly. He said, "You so-'n'-so, you're messing with the wrong old man this time."

After a couple of jerks and kicks, this old horse just stood quivering and watching Apache. He climbed in the saddle, over and undered him with the reins, and they disappeared into the grease wood and mesquite in a run.

About 15 minutes later, horse and rider reappeared. The horse was lathered up pretty good but came trotting in under total control.

Apache wasn't cruel to the horse, but he sure made him understand who the boss was. A few more sessions, and the horse came around and earned his keep.

Shootin' the Bull

Apache and Joy hadn't owned the new ranch very long when they started having problems with a big black bull jumping the fence and getting in with their cows. This bull weighed 1,500 or 1,600 pounds and wasn't worried about a little fence or two.

There was an absentee landowner on that neighboring ranch, and he had stock that had never been branded or even gathered.

I got a phone call early one morning, and a familiar voice said, "You want to come out and shoot a bull for me."

I said, "Well, I'm probably better at shooting them than I am a roping them. What's up?"

Apache replied, "I've got a new dart gun that's supposed to

knock out a rhino, and I want to try it out on this bull that keeps jumping my fence."

I said, "Well, I sure can't pass that up." And we made plans for the following weekend.

So Blain Ward, Apache, and I set out early the following Saturday to find this black bull, riding some new young horses Apache had just traded for. We located him pretty quick, and Apache handed me the dart gun.

We started sneaking through the brush on foot toward the bull. The only thing between us and old toro was ocotillo and grease wood, and I whispered to Apache, "What do we do if HE comes after US?"

He replied, "Well, first, don't miss. And second, run like hell if you do."

He spotted us and kept moving out of range of the dart gun.

Finally, we had started walking back to the truck and our horses when Blain came riding up on his horse.

He said, "Give me that gun. I've always wanted to try this." He took the gun and spurred his horse into a dead run right at the bull. He rode up next to the running bull like Buffalo Bill and tried to shoot him from horseback.

The dart glanced off, so Blain rode back and pitched me the gun.

Apache and I were getting our horses out of the trailer; and, un-coiling his rope, Blain took off after the bull.

Blain Ward sitting on the tied-down bull that he tried to shoot
with a tranquilizer gun, "Buffalo Bill style"

By the time we caught up, Blain had the bull roped in a little
clearing pretty near the road. He hollered, "Somebody get a rope
on that bull's hind legs. I don't think this little horse I'm on has done
much of this."

Apache yelled, "Quick, change horses with me, Don. I'm riding a
complete idiot, and he's never had anything roped off him."

That never seemed to bother Apache before, but I jumped off and
swapped horses with him. One thing I knew for sure, this was no time
for amateurs. If someone didn't get that bull heeled pretty fast, things
were going to turn ugly.

As we traded mounts, I grabbed my pigging string off my saddle. I
tied Apache's horse to a bush away from the ruckus and waited while
Apache caught the bull's hind feet. When they stretched the bull out,
I ran in to tie him.

Blain jumped off his horse, and we met at the bull. We got him tied by the time two other men had driven up with our truck and trailer and a little Toyota pickup.

They backed the trailer up to the bull, and Blain and I put our ropes around the bull's horns. We ran the ropes through the trailer and pulled them taut with our horses.

Apache untied the bull; but he was worn out and wasn't moving a muscle. Our horses couldn't pull hard enough to get the bull's dead weight up and into the trailer.

Apache said, "Hold on, boys. I've got just the tool for this job." He went over to the little four-cylinder Toyota pickup and backed it up to the side of the trailer.

There was a big rope in the back of the truck that must have been used to tie battleships with. He tied it around the bull's horns, ran it through the trailer, and tied it to the bumper of the Toyota.

We got our ropes and horses out of the way...way out of the way...and Apache gassed the Toyota.

The bull didn't budge.

Apache backed up all the way to the trailer, put about 10 feet of slack in the rope, and floor-boarded it.

The truck stopped, but the bull moved about a foot.

Apache said, "Blain, you and Don hold that bull's head up, so it'll go in the trailer the next time I hit the end of the rope."

I looked at Blain and said, "His feet aren't tied any more. If he gets his second wind about the time we grab his horns, it could get exciting real fast."

Blain said, "Yep, and Adams will just drag all three of us into the trailer and slam the gate."

We each grabbed a horn and lifted. Blain hollered, "Gas it," and the little Toyota hit the end of the rope.

Old toro slid right up into the trailer like he was on a carnival ride.

Just another day at the ranch.

Wild Bulls and Deer Feeders

In 2007, my wife Pam and I moved from Dripping Springs, Texas, to a place we bought south of Alpine. We were building our own home there and were working seven days a week trying to finish it.

Apache called one morning and said, "You need a break from all that hard work. A feller named Ken leased the ranch next to me, and he needs some wild cattle caught. Come on over Friday night, and we'll go after them at first light Saturday."

I did need a break from the craziness of the building project and sure didn't want to miss an Adams' wild-cow gathering, so I said I'd be there. Apache's brother David also came down from Ft. Worth to join in the fun. Ken's father-in-law was a cowboy, and he agreed to help.

Ken was leasing the ranch for a hunting operation, and the owner had shipped all of the cattle off the place. But there were two bulls and a cow that they couldn't gather that were playing havoc with all of the new deer feeders. If we couldn't rope them, Ken said he was going to have to shoot them.

Ken said he'd seen fresh tracks in one of the pastures, so we rode out at first light and pretty soon spotted the cattle. The two bulls went one way, and the cow another. Apache yelled, "David and I'll get the bulls. You two go after the cow."

Everybody took off hell for leather.

The fellow I was with threw and missed the cow. I missed my loop, too, and the cow got on the fight and charged the other fellow's horse. When the cow hit his horse, he dropped a loop right over her head, and I rode in and roped a hind foot. We tied her down and went to check on the other guys.

Apache and David had caught the smaller of the two bulls and had him tied.

Ken brought the trailer, and we loaded the cow first. Just as we were pulling up to load the bull, he got his feet loose and jumped up and took off running. We got him roped again and finally loaded in the trailer with the cow.

We put the cow and bull in some pens, and after lunch we started trying to find the bigger bull. This was a 30,000-acre ranch, and that bull knew we were after him. He had gone undercover.

For over two hours we looked for tracks. We finally cut his trail, and Apache went into full-blown Indian mode. "Everybody stay behind me, so you don't mess up the tracks I'm following," he whispered. "And no talking. That bull is like a whitetail deer. He'll hear us and sneak off, and we'll never see him."

Everyone had their ropes down and a loop built as we rode slowly along.

We got to a place where the bull had cut back on his own trail, and Apache said, "Spread out and look under every bush, but don't ride ahead of where I am. That bull's laying under one of these cedars, and he's ready to bulldoze somebody."

In a few minutes, Apache started waving us over to where he was. He pointed at a cedar tree that draped to the ground. He still couldn't see the bull; but he had seen his tracks go in, and they didn't come out.

All of a sudden, the cedar exploded, and that bull came out like Seabiscuit from the starting gate. In a cloud of dust, we all took off after the bull, ropes swinging in every direction.

As usual, Apache was "pushing on the reins" a little harder than the rest of us, and he got the bull roped. David ran in and got one hind foot, but they couldn't get the bull down, and he was pulling their horses around pretty hard.

Apache said, "Somebody get another rope on the bull's head."

In the chaos of a pissed-off, 1,700-pound bull in the middle of two 30-foot ropes with horses trying to keep the ropes tight, the other fellow finally got another rope on the bull's head.

I was trying to get another hind foot, so we could stretch him out but somehow managed to snag a front foot in my rope. Now we had two ropes on his head, one on a hind foot, and one on a front foot.

Apache hollered above the mayhem, "Don, put slack in your

rope, flip it over David and his horse, and get it diagonally over the bull's back."

I got that done, and he said, "Now, ride off as hard as you can, and flip this big bastard over."

I did; and when I hit the end of my rope, it just stopped my horse. The bull was so big and strong, he could hold his foot down and keep his balance.

We messed with that big sucker for an hour and never got him on the ground.

Apache finally said, "These horses are starting to give out. Ken, back the trailer up as close as you can to the bull."

Apache had a winch mounted in the front of his trailer. He said, "Ken, pull that winch cable out and wrap that chain on the end of the cable around the bull's horns."

Ken was in a bad position because even with four ropes on him, the bull wasn't under total control. Ken was finally able to pitch the chain over the bull's horns.

Apache yelled, "Hit the power on that winch, and don't stop until that bull's head is sucked up against the front trailer wall."

There were 4 worn-out horses and 4 worn-out men, but that bull was still fighting when we got him loaded.

Most people have no idea how fast, strong, and athletic an animal that big can be; or how many chances there are to get killed in a situation like that.

Roping Cows in Town

In August of 2010, I was helping Apache gather and sort some cattle on his ranch south of Ft. Stockton. We gathered a bunch of cows and calves, weaned off the calves and penned them, and turned the mothers back out to pasture.

Apache picked out 8 cows that he wanted to load and move to a lease place he has. We loaded them in the trailer, and two men that work for him were going to bring them in for the night to some pens he keeps in Ft. Stockton.

We tended to a couple of things and then went to Apache's house in town.

About 9 P.M. the phone rang. One of his men said the trailer had burned out a bearing, thrown a wheel off, and was sitting in the middle of the road loaded with cows.

We drove my truck and trailer out to where they were stranded. We got the cows moved from one trailer to the other in the dark, and then got the cows to the pens and unloaded them.

The next morning, we headed out early to load the cows and take them to the lease pasture. As we were loading them, one of the cows managed to jump the fence and took off.

These pens are in the city limits of Ft. Stockton and in an area where people have small 2- to 10-acre places with lots of old fences, brush, and tall grass.

Apache said, "Don, you and Edgar get on your horses, and I'm going to drive the pickup around and talk to folks. We've got to find that cow in all this mess and get her roped."

Most people in that part of town speak Spanish, and it became a sort of charreada[37] event, with people standing in the back of pickups and shouting instructions as to the location of the fence-jumping, brush-busting cow.

This went on for three hours. When the cow came to a fence, she either jumped it or just went through it. We had to go around the fences on our horses and then start the search all over again in the brush.

Finally, Edgar saw the cow hidden in a big clump of mesquite, right next to a paved road.

Apache jumped out of the truck, looked up at me, and said, "Don, we probably only have one chance at this cow, and I'd like to take it. Can I use your horse?"

I was happy to hand him the reins and the rope and pull up the cinch on my little black horse Prieto for him. I eased around behind

---

37   charreada - A Mexican rodeo.

the mesquite on foot and ran the cow out right in front of him.

Cow, horse, and rider took off in a dead run right down the middle of the paved road.

The cow was fast, and Apache had to run her several blocks. Luckily, there were fences on both sides of the road, so it was just a straight-on horse race. But a paved road is a hell of a bad place to have to run a horse.

Just as they were almost out of sight, I saw Apache throw, wave slack, and shut Prieto down.

The cow was jerking and flopping on the rope, so I jumped in the truck and roared down the road with the trailer. We got another rope on her, ran the ropes through the sides of the trailer, and loaded her up.

Apache handed me my horse, and said, "Damn, I love it when a plan comes together."

Just as we got her loaded and started back to the pens, Pete called from the ranch. He said that some bulls had broken the gate down into the pen where the weaned calves were, so they had all raced back to their mothers.

Apache closed his cell phone, looked at me with a big smile, and said, "Just another typical day on the Adams outfit!"

Apache (in the black hat) being inducted into
The Big Bend Cowboy Hall of Fame in 2009

PART THREE
RECOLLECTIONS

Stories from a Few Friends

He thumped him in the shoulders

and spurred him when he whirled,

and showed us flunky punchers

he was the wolf of this old world.

          —Anonymous, from "The Zebra Dun"

I thought you readers might find it interesting to hear some of Apache's stories from the perspective of his friends, the people who have worked and ridden with him over the years.

—The Author

Joe Richardson

Retired school teacher, cowboy, gun trader; grew up in Alpine

One Sunday morning, a bunch of us were drinking coffee out at the Sunday House Café in Alpine. Old Bill Madden, who was a big horse trader, asked Apache if he was busy that morning.

Apache said he wasn't, and Bill asked him if he'd mind coming out to his place and riding a mule that Bill had traded for. I knew the kinds of deals Bill got into, so I asked if I could tag along.

We got out there, and Bill had this little chunky, wild-eyed mule in a pen. She was spooky as hell and didn't want anybody near her.

Apache got a saddle on her, but the cantle was poking right straight up in the air because that little mule was humped up and ready for a fight. Before I could blink, Apache pulled the mule around to him and was on her back, and she went to pitching around that little pen.

Apache told me to open the gate to the alley down the side of the pens. She pitched all the way down the alley and into the water lot.

When he'd want her to turn left, he'd take his hat in his right hand and kinda fan her on the right side of her face. He'd do the same thing on the other side, and the whole time she never quit pitching.

Apache rode her that way back up the alley and back into the pen he started in. Then he spun her around and jumped off on the ground. He looked at Bill and me and said, "Yeah, I believe she'll make a pretty good little mule."

I guarantee you, I wouldn't have fed her two grains of oats or given a plug nickel for her. But Apache would have probably taken her out that afternoon and worked cattle on her.

Another time, I saw Dogie Delaney talking to some stranger in a pickup where I was filling up with gas. The guy drove off, and Dogie walked over and asked me if I wanted to see a little fun. He said this guy was supposed to meet Apache to look at a horse to buy. They'd gotten their wires crossed, and the guy had been waiting in the wrong place for an hour.

Apache had sent Dogie around town to try to find the guy; and when he found him, the fellow was plenty hot because of the wait. He told Dogie he was going to find this Apache guy and give him a piece of his mind.

Dogie said, "This ought to be good." We jumped in the truck and headed out to where Apache was to watch the fun.

This fellow got out of the truck cussing Apache about having to sit around for an hour.

Apache had just gotten over the flu and looked like death warmed over. He came out of his truck in a heartbeat and said something like, "You SOB, don't buy this horse if you don't want him. But don't you go to cussing me, or I'll whip your butt all over this pasture."

The guy bought the horse. Hell, I think he was scared not to.

Steve Stumberg

Retired rancher well-known for his trapping skills; grew up and went to school in Marathon with Apache and David Adams

When Apache and David were in high school, they decided they were going to be world-famous bronc riders. So they bought or traded somebody out of two bucking horses and took them to The River Ranch.

They didn't have an arena, but they had this old goat pen they were going to use to practice in.

The only problem was that there was a shed right in the middle of the pen.

They had one of the Mexicans that their dad had working on the ranch spend the day raking rocks and carrying them out of the pen.

Branding crew on the Adams Ranch, circa 2009; left to right: Blain Ward, the author, Pat Yeager, Dusty Roller, Frankie Galvan, Justin Clinton, Apache (nursing a broken pelvis)

Then on practice day, they had the fellow stand under the shed. They told him that if one of the horses bucked toward the shed, to shoo him away so that the horses wouldn't buck up under the shed.

Sure enough, Apache's horse bucked out of the little chute they'd scrapped together and headed right straight for the shed. When he got close, this Mexican boy stepped out with his steel rake and hit the horse right between the ears as hard as he could.

Well, the horse went down like he was shot.

Apache jumped clear of the horse, walked up to this poor Mexican fellow, and said, "If that horse dies, you do, too!"

Luckily, the horse made it, but Apache and David never did make the National Finals.

Later on in life when I was ranching, Apache and I made some kind of a crazy trade on a cow. I don't remember what I got, but Apache got a cow from me.

When he came to the ranch to get her, I'd already picked out the wildest cow I had, and I damn sure wanted to get rid of her.

Apache showed up in his pickup that he'd stuck some old side boards on. We were going to load this crazy cow in it and then tie her down so she couldn't jump out.

He backed his truck up to my loading chute, and we finally got the cow separated from the bunch and into the chute. She jumped into the bed of his truck and immediately ran one of her horns through the rear window, smashing it out. We finally got her tied down somehow.

He had planned to take the cow back to his ranch; but he said she was so crazy, he didn't want her in his herd.

He just took off for the 250-mile drive to San Angelo to take her to the auction.

It was the dead of winter and cold as hell, and there he was, driving down the highway with no back window, and a wild cow flopping around in the back of the truck.

But it didn't seem to bother him much.

Dusty Roller

The grandson Apache raised; has "enjoyed" many adventures with his grandpa

After Grandpa broke his pelvis in 2008 in another horse wreck, he was pretty much of a mess for almost two years. Once the bones all grew back together, the doctor finally told him he could ride again if he could stand to sit on a saddle.

He was having a hard time walking, and we sure didn't think he could ride, but he was determined to try.

One morning when he and Grandma got up around 6 A.M., he decided he was going to try and sit on the trophy saddle I won riding saddle broncs. It was on a saddle stand in the living room.

Grandma helped him get on, and then she went in to make coffee.

Apache heeling a calf at Adams Ranch branding, 2010.
Grandson Dusty waiting to flank the calf

It hurt him to sit in it, so he tried to get off by himself. When he leaned to the left to get off, the saddle rolled on the stand, and he ended up in the middle of the floor with the saddle and stand on top of him.

I was still asleep in my room, and Grandma came in and woke me up telling me that I had to help her get the saddle off Grandpa and get him to his chair. I didn't know what was going on until I went into the living room and saw him all tangled up with the saddle.

He finally got a hip replacement and was able to ride again. But I still like to remind him that he got bucked off the saddle stand in the living room.

Pat Yeager

One of the "boys" who has ridden with Apache since he was a kid; has been part of lots of wild cow roping expeditions as well as helping with cow works on ranches Apache has leased or owned over the years

Apache called me one day and told me he had a cow down at Pinto Canyon that he thought was prolapsed[38], and he sure needed to find her and tend to her. It was summer and miserably hot, and Pinto Canyon was like an oven.

We took off horseback and looked for the cow most of the morning. We finally found her; but she was too far gone for us to do anything to help her, so we had to put her out of her misery. Then we had a pretty long and hot ride back to the truck.

When we finally got there about 2:00, Apache said, "I'll bet you're ready for lunch, and I've got us fixed up."

He got a little ice chest out of the truck, and we went over to the creek that was still running and got a long drink of cool water.

Then we got up under a nice shade tree, and Apache opened the cooler. He was on one of his diets, and all he had was a 6-pack of chocolate Slim Fast. That was it!

He told me to help myself. I kept thinking maybe we should go back and cut a rib eye off the dead cow!

Frankie Galvan

Grew up in Ft. Stockton in a family of cowboys and team ropers; another one of Apache's "boys" who has made a lot of horse tracks with him

I was about 18 years old and had roped a lot of steers in the arena, but never roped a cow out in the pasture. Apache took me with him

---

38   prolapse - A severe condition where the uterus of the cow slips and protrudes out of the vaginal opening.

down to Pinto Canyon to help clean out some wild cattle before he put his cows out down there.

I was riding a horse of Apache's named Captain, and we had a little bunch of cows gathered and were trying to move them.

Frankie Galvan and Apache ahorseback, 2010

Apache rode up and said, "Boys, I don't care what else happens today, but that damn high-horned brindle Braford cow in this bunch is going to town."

We got the bunch to the pens, but she broke off right before we got to the gate and hid in some brush. We shut the gate and all went to find her and rope her.

As we were loping back to find the cow, Apache looked down at my saddle and noticed that my rope wasn't tied to the horn. He said, "You gonna dally if you rope this cow?"

I said, "Well yeah, that's how I planned on stopping her once I got her roped."

He said, "You're riding my horse, and roping my cow, on my place. If you want her, then tie that rope to your horn and go get her. If you don't, then just leave your rope hanging on your saddle and let us get her."

I said, "Alrighty, boss, whatever you say." I tied on and ended up roping her.

Once I got her stopped and my horse facing her, I looked at Apache and said, "OK, I got her roped. Now what the hell do I do with her?"

They helped me get her tied down, and we got a trailer to her and loaded her up.

That was the first of many cows I roped riding with him.

We've had a lot of good times and a lot of near disasters together, but it's all been interesting.

David Adams

Apache's younger brother by two years; a graduate of Texas A&M University, retired businessman and investor; a good hand with a horse and a rope

Growing up as Apache's younger brother was a challenge. About the only days we didn't have a fight with each other were the days we were fighting some other kids. I don't think he ever threw a rock in his life that didn't hit me in the head. It's amazing we survived our childhood on that old River Ranch, but somehow we did.

We were always into something, and one of our favorite things was to jump out of the hay loft of the barn into a big pile of hay about 10 feet below. One day just as I was jumping, Apache swung one of the wooden stall gates under me. It caught me right under the chin.

If I'd been two inches shorter, it would have broken my neck. As it was, it just ripped a gap open under my chin, and I donated another pint of blood to the ranch before Mother could get me patched back together.

Dad had a mule named Alacron, which is Spanish for scorpion. He could "sting" you with a foot before you could think if you were anywhere near him, and Apache was the only one who could ride him.

Once he was mounted, old Alacron was a heck of a mule, and Apache could go anywhere or rope anything off him.

One day I heard Apache hollering and cussing, and I ran to see what had happened. He was shoeing Alacron, and I found him bent over moaning and rubbing his knee like he'd broken it. When I asked him what was wrong, he said, "That damn mule kicked me right behind the ear."

I said, "Well, if he kicked you behind the ear, why are you rubbing your knee?"

Apache said, "'Cause I swung the horseshoe rasp at him when he kicked me, missed him, and hit myself right on the kneecap. It hurts more than my ear."

We were out looking for some cattle one day; Apache was on Alacron, and I was on one of the horses. We were up in some high rimrock, and there was a bluff up there that was 500 or 600 feet straight down.

For some reason, Alacron spooked and cold-jawed and headed straight for that bluff with Apache pulling as hard as he could trying to get him turned.

I managed to get up beside him on my horse and started whipping Alacron over the head with my rope and trying to turn him.

When he finally turned, we were way too close to the edge, and it scared us both pretty good. That was one we wouldn't have survived if we'd gone over.

Having Apache for a brother has sure made life interesting. There haven't been many dull moments when he was involved.

Preston Adams

Elba Adams' son who grew up with Apache and David; not a big man and, now in his 70s, seems like a nice, gentle fellow; but Apache says, "He was the fastest, meanest, toughest kid to come out of Marathon, and a heck of a football player to boot"

There used to be a filling station in Marathon where the "Coffee Shop" is now. Apache and I got into a little ruckus down there one night with a couple of local boys. I had one of the guy's hands slammed under the lid of an old Dr. Pepper cold box, and his other arm pinned behind his back. I was sitting on the lid of the box, so he couldn't get his hand out and working on his face with my free hand.

Apache was doing a pretty good job on another one until the guy's buddy came up from behind and pinned Apache's arms down. Then that ol' boy moved Apache's nose over to the far right side of his face if I remember right. We ended up whipping 'em, but Apache sure had a mess for a nose for a few weeks.

When we all lived down on The River Ranch, our daddies had lion traps set all down through a big canyon.

Apache and I were only 6 or 7, and they'd send us ahorseback to check the trap line; but they said we might get excited and shoot each other if we saw a lion, so they sent us bare-handed. We were supposed to ride back and let them know if a trap was missing, so they could follow the drag and kill the lion. Hell, I think that might be the most scared I ever was in my life.

We'd ride down that narrow canyon and see a lion behind every bush. I'd catch myself years later riding through there looking left and right all the time.

People don't even let their kids walk to school by themselves nowadays. They'd have heart failure if they saw how we grew up.

Ted Gray

An indisputable legend in West Texas; came to Alpine as a young boy in 1938 with a few dollars in his pocket; worked his way up to running the massive Kokernot o6 Ranch and on to owning large ranches himself and being successful in the oil business; the epitome of the self-made man and respected as one of the wildest men horseback to ever cowboy in the Big Bend country; Apache and Ted are old friends now; and as a young man himself, Apache worked for Ted on the o6. Ted allowed me to excerpt the following from his book Shades of the West.*

Apache Adams was a wild young boy when he worked for me. When he first arrived at the ranch, he was wearing house shoes. Applying to be a cowboy, he sure wasn't dressed for the job, but he did make an immediate impression. It was obvious that Apache needed the job, and I hired him on the spot.

It was a bit unusual, but right after being hired, he asked me for a loan. I loaned him some money, and he assured me he'd pay me back when he could.

Apache had a talent for breaking horses, and he worked with the young horses. About two months after he started working, I had to leave the ranch to be gone for 10 days.

"Apache," I called to him, "I want to tell you what you need to be doing while I'm gone. You'll need to turn the colts out, ride my mount of horses, and keep the worms out of the cattle. We have lots of worms, and you'll need to really keep after them on good broke horses, not those broncs."

Instructions given, I left. After being gone for the 10 days, I returned to find that my horses hadn't been ridden. Apache was no where to be found.

I saddled my horse and went down through the ranch.

There were places in the pasture that looked like Apache had put in a farm! He had been roping those cows off of those raw broncs!

There were trenches cut into the soil from the fighting hooves of the cows and the bronc, and places round the waterings in the pasture looked like they had been plowed.

And there he was, still roping the bulls and cows off those colts.

Apache made one wild cowboy, and a good one.

EPILOGUE

Apache Adams is certainly not the only good cowboy in the Big Bend region of Texas. But he is considered a sort of "living legend" by many respected ranchers and cowboys who know him.

In many ways, Apache truly represents the end of an era in American history. He lived most of the first 20 years of his life on a ranch without electricity or running water. The nearest town was 70 miles away by dirt road, and daily ranch life was not much different than it had been on such places for the previous hundred years.

His life has spanned a time when automobiles were a secondary means of transportation to horses, to a time when he was flying his own airplane. He has gone from the days of cattle being driven to railheads to seeing them sold via video and computers to buyers thousands of miles away.

It is my hope that these stories of his life will give future generations a glimpse of what ranch life was truly like, at least in the wilds of far West Texas. Or as John Wayne once put it, "Back when the men were men, and the women loved 'em for it!"

ACKNOWLEDGEMENTS

Back in the mid-1990s, Marion Barthelme, who is the owner of Pinto Canyon Ranch with her husband Jeff Fort, gave Apache Adams a small cassette tape recorder. She asked him to keep it in his truck and to record all of his stories as he was driving around.

Marion had planned to write a magazine article or a book using the tapes; but other issues came up, and she never did. She was kind enough to give me the tapes, and they are the basis for the book.

I had a lot of help and encouragement putting the book together. My wife Pam, who has a degree in English, kept me on track. My daughter Melissa, who is a graphic artist, shared her talent for the cover. My friend David Marion Wilkinson, who is a wonderful writer, gave me sage advice and patiently answered my many emails. Friend and book editor Annie Bright was kind enough to read the manuscript and provide honest comments. Patricia Saunders did a very professional job of editing and bringing the project together.

All of the folks who added their stories to the mix were great to work with and fun to talk to.

And of course Apache Adams has allowed me to tell his story as well as share in "the fun."

Don Cadden

©2010 Scott Van Osdol, www.vanosdol.com

Born in Gonzales, Texas, in 1946, Don grew up in the rural community of Del Valle. He graduated from Southwest Texas State University and served in the military. He lived most of his adult life in the Austin and Dripping Springs areas, but also spent a lot of time in the brush country of South Texas and in the Big Bend area of West Texas.

He and his wife Pam Cook live on a small place south of Alpine, Texas. There, they run a few cows, and Don day-works on various ranches in the area. Don and Pam have four grown children and two grandchildren. Since 1990, he has performed music and poetry at cowboy gatherings around The West.